MW01171602

THE
TIME TRAVEL
INTERPRETATION OF THE
BIBLE

Jonathan W. Tooker

Contents

Psalm 93:1-2 (NIV)

1   The Lord reigns, he is robed in majesty;
the Lord is robed in majesty and armed with
strength; indeed, the world is established,
firm and secure.
2   Your throne was established long ago;
you are from all eternity.

1. Introduction

This book is a companion to the Bible. It does not contain a full analysis which would entail a review of every verse, cover to cover. Rather, this book is a tool for Bible study, and it stands as an independent thesis as well. The main theme presented here is that God's work is the work of ages, not the work of a moment, because he uses time travel constrained by the laws of physics. This contrasts a prevailing view that God is omnipotent as if by magic and could get all of his work done in a moment but does not, for some reason. By his mastery of time travel via technology that will exist in the future, God's work is written across the ages of the Earth.

Before moving on from this introductory section, the reader is encouraged to read The First Book of Moses, called Genesis. Even if the reader was already familiarized through a previous introduction to the material, the reader is encouraged to stop reading this book and reread Genesis. With Genesis fresh in the reader's mind, we will make the case that Jacob, a.k.a. Israel, is Satan. In this view, we will suppose that God wanted Abraham to kill his son Isaac to prevent Isaac from becoming the father of Satan. Everyone familiar with the idea of time travel has heard a question, "If you had a time machine, would you go back and kill so and so?" We will frame the issue of God's edict against Isaac in that context. We will also suggest that God stayed Abraham's hand above his son because God himself (or Jesus for whom we will offer a time travel interpretation later) is the descen-

dant of Abraham through his grandson Satan, as below
in Revelation 22. By preventing the birth of Satan, God
would have executed the grandfather paradox[1] on himself. Physics suggests that this is not possible. Killing an
ancestor before one's birth is not allowed.

> ## Revelation 22:16 (NIV)
>
> **16** "I, Jesus, have sent my angel to give you this
> testimony for the churches. I am the Root and
> the Offspring of David, and the bright morning
> star."

The morning star is the devil. We will continue to cite
the circumstance referenced in Revelation 22 as integral
to the crux of the matter in the battle of good versus evil.

In this interpretation of the Bible, we will diverge
from a popular conception that God is essentially magical in nature. Instead, we will constrain the Lord according to the laws of physics. Then we will arrange
omnipotence, omniscience, and omnipresence in good order so that these traits are not lost. Rather, they will be
understood from an unfamiliar point of view.

Notes

[1] "Grandfather paradox," https://en.wikipedia.org/wiki/
Grandfather_paradox.

2. Proof That God Exists

The lack of a proof of the existence of God is sometimes taken as an axiom of the religious systems of the Abrahamic faiths, and here we do not categorically prove the existence of God. However, we will show that if time travel exists, then a supernatural supreme being of some sort necessarily exists as well. We will make the case that this supreme being is the Almighty God of Abraham: the Sovereign Lord. The proof proceeds as follows.

It is well known in Einstein's theory of relativity that timelines are allowed to loop back on themselves,[2] and that, therefore, time travel is possible in theory. It is also known that nothing more than the unification of classical electromagnetism and gravitation stands in the way of an electrical antenna capable of producing such timelines (in theory.) So, to proceed with the proof, we will suppose that this technical feat of unification will be accomplished at some point in the future.

If there exists a time machine, then there exists a time travel organization employing people in roles related to time travel. Within the attendant administrative complex, there exists a console at which people operate the device itself. The nature of time travel is such that anyone operating a time machine has the ability to rewrite history. In a practical sense, whatever changes are made by one person can be overwritten by another. We will frame the contention over what changes ought to be written into history as contention between a day shift and a night shift employed at the console.

During the day, time travel work is done. When the night shift comes on and the day shift sleeps, any work done during the day can be overwritten. Throughout time, one imagines that day and night, and back and forth, one shift overwrites another as the day manager and the night manager have different thoughts on what the course of history ought to have been. Time goes by and both shifts' managers retire. The technicians retire. In every new generation, new people come in to man the console. Perhaps different generations fight over different things. The subject of the tit for tat between day and night changes over time while the contention that one shift can always overwrite the previous shift remains. Someone else will always come along thinking history should have unfolded according to their own vision, not someone else's.

Who gets to decide what the real course of history was? Every day shift is followed by a night shift and every night shift by a day shift, so neither will ever get the final word. Therefore, the real course of immutable history that we all share must be the limit of an infinite number of changes. The history that we all share is the final word once all of the time travel work has been done. Since there will always have been a finite number of human generations following the construction of the first time machine, and since the men of each generation will work only a finite number of shifts during their lives, humans will never be able to write the last of an infinite number of changes. If the last word cannot be had by any mortal, then it must be had by some supernatural entity. It is the thesis of the present interpretation of the Bible that the final course of history is determined by the will of God. We do not conflate the name of God with some ambiguous entity of a metaphysical variety. Instead, we suppose that the God of Abraham rules over time. The Bible is the chronicle of his works. Here, we seat God on the throne of his eternal glory at timelike infinity:[3] the end of time, a place that no mortal will ever reach.

Notes

[2] "Closed timelike curve," https://en.wikipedia.org/wiki/Closed_timelike_curve.

[3] "Penrose diagram," https://en.wikipedia.org/wiki/Penrose_diagram.

3. The Past, Present, and Future

For the purposes of the time travel interpretation, we will propose an alternative translation of some ancient language appearing throughout the Bible. Heaven should be read as *the future*, the earth should be read as *the present*, and the depths or the seas should be read as *the past*. In this way, God lives in heaven because God lives in the future. Prophets are able to tell the course of events to come when God sends his word from the future. God sends word via the angels which are his time travel *agents*. The Kingdom of God is in heaven because the moment of Satan's ultimate defeat is written into history at a later date than were the promises of that kingdom's coming. Religious teaching to believe in God and to hold on and be strong is well motivated when the knowledge of the wisdom of that course comes from those who have already seen God's victory at the end of the age. We will continue to motivate these concepts in the following sections.

Matthew 6:9-13 (NIV)

9 This, then, is how you should pray:

> "'Our Father in heaven,
> hallowed be your name,
10   your kingdom come,
> your will be done,

> [*in the present*] as it is in [*the future*].
> 11 Give us today our daily bread.
> 12 And forgive us our debts,
>   as we also have forgiven our debtors.
> 13 And lead us not into temptation,
>   but deliver us from the evil one.'["]

We will give a great deal of attention to the idea that Abraham's grandson Israel is the evil one mentioned in this famous prayer.

4. The Parable of the Weeds

We take it for granted that good intentions for revisions to history will always dominate on long timescales. Each time evil is written into history, the descendants of the author of that evil will always fall under the spell of it on sufficiently long timescales. Therefore, appealing to the self-interest of the agents at the time console without any reference to traits of nobility and honor, traits which surely exist, agents will be more disposed to overwrite evil changes. People do not want evil for themselves or their children, in general. When good is written into history and it spreads through time, people are not offended when it falls on their children. In this way, good is favored over evil across the annals of time. For this reason, God is good. It is the intention for good which survives all the way to infinity, and we have taken God's will as the will which survives until the end. God determines the course of history. Evil cannot make it all the way until the end, regardless of its profit motive or other incentive, because profits always fade, and then the descendants at later times are left with evil. Any wickedness written into history inevitably becomes a wickedness befalling everyone else. Evil in history is likely to be a blight in the minds of those in the future with an advantage of hindsight. For this reason, the righteous among later generations are more inclined to overwrite evil with righteousness than are the wicked to overwrite righteousness with evil.

Matthew 13:24-30 (NIV)

24 Jesus told them another parable: "The kingdom of heaven is like a man who sowed good seed in his field. 25 But while everyone was sleeping, his enemy came and sowed weeds among the wheat, and went away. 26 When the wheat sprouted and formed heads, then the weeds also appeared.

27 "The owner's servants came to him and said, 'Sir, didn't you sow good seed in your field? Where then did the weeds come from?'

28 "'An enemy did this,' he replied.

"The servants asked him, 'Do you want us to go and pull them up?'

29 "'No,' he answered, 'because while you are pulling the weeds, you may uproot the wheat with them. 30 Let both grow together until the harvest. At that time I will tell the harvesters: First collect the weeds and tie them in bundles to be burned; then gather the wheat and bring it into my barn.'"

As the limit of an infinite number of revisions, the real course of history would ideally reflect the good intentions sown into the field of time by the allegorical day shift. After good intentions were written, however, the night shift came on and wrote wicked things into history. By the time history was well underway, there were good things and evil things, and the state of the world did not on its surface reflect God's benevolence or the goodness of his creation. Long after the weeds were planted, time travel was invented. *Agents*, or angels, were organized for the administration and operation of the time machine. Looking back through history as in verse 26, it was obvious that the time machine was being used for good and for evil. A war was fought in the future, and God was the winner. God survives to timelike infinity, not Satan, because God was victorious in the war whose stakes could have been nothing less than the seat in that eternal throne.

In verse 27, the time agents asked God, "Should we try to undo these evil things that Satan has written into history?" God told them, "No, because while you are rewriting history you might mess it up worse than Satan already did. Leave the good and the bad as they are until the time of the harvest." The time of the harvest is the coming of the Kingdom of God. It is his final victory over the wickedness written into the world by his enemy the devil. At that time, on the Day of the Lord, also called the Day of Judgment, God will send out his servants to destroy the remnant of Satan that has flourished across history. He will kill them for the sins of their ancestors. Then God will establish his kingdom for the care and advancement of the remnant who will enjoy creation as God intended from the beginning.

Isaiah 14:21-27 (NIV)

21   Prepare a place to slaughter his children
      for the sins of their ancestors;
  they are not to rise to inherit the land
      and cover the earth with their cities.

22 "I will rise up against them,"
      declares the Lord Almighty.
  "I will wipe out Babylon's name and survivors,
      her offspring and descendants,"
        declares the Lord.

23 "I will turn her into a place for owls
      and into swampland;
  I will sweep her with the broom of destruction,"
      declares the Lord Almighty.

24 The Lord Almighty has sworn,

  "Surely, as I have planned, so it will be,
      and as I have purposed, so it will happen.

25 I will crush the Assyrian in my land;
      on my mountains I will trample him down.
  His yoke will be taken from my people,
      and his burden removed from their shoulders."

26 This is the plan determined for the whole world;

11

> this is the hand stretched out over all nations.
>
> 27 For the Lord Almighty has purposed, and who can thwart him?
>
> His hand is stretched out, and who can turn it back?

Isaiah 14 describes what will happen at the time of the harvest. While we will reanalyze these verses in Section 13, the context to be understood is that Babylon and Assyria were kingdoms seeded and fostered by factions vying against God in time. God does not destroy these enemy kingdoms in their nascency. It is God's plan to wait until the end of the age at which time the Kingdom of God will be the only kingdom. In verse 27, we see that no one can turn back the Lord's hand because he acts last from his throne at the end of time. Anything done by anyone other than the Lord must have been done at some finite time before timelike infinity. As a consequence, God and any person alive at a later time will have agency to overwrite those actions. This is the supremacy of God's throne: when God acts, no one can undo it.

The Parable of the Weeds illuminates an often asked question about the nature of God. Sometimes one asks, "If God is real, then how could he have let little Sally's puppy get run over by that car?" The parable shows that God is not a micromanager. It is the Lord's wisdom that it is better to leave not only rival kingdoms until the end, but even to leave Satan's most vile works unchallenged until the end. The wisdom is clear. Satan was not strong enough to defeat God, and God will not shake the foundations of his kingdom any more than Satan already has. If something is such that it would prevent God's eventual victory over Satan, such as, perhaps, if the Israelites had remained slaves in Egypt without the ten plagues heralded by Moses and the dashing of Pharaoh's army in the Red Sea, then God will intercede. If something is not such that leaving it untouched will destroy God's kingdom, then God's wisdom is that it is better to leave it be. By the end, Satan was not strong enough to write God's defeat into history.

While it is offensive to some to think that God chooses not to address certain evils, even the most wicked evils, this represents a noble quality of leadership which is considered desirable even in the halls of earthly power. This is the sort of big picture thinking appropriate for effectiveness as the master of creation reigning on high forever from the seat at timelike infinity. If God intercedes to stop Sally's puppy from getting run over, then the butterfly effect[4] will be implemented. It cannot be known ahead of time if the effect will be significant or insignificant. The different future which follows from the history in which Sally's dog lives will always have many new events, and each will spawn a new butterfly effect. While some of those changes might not cause the destruction of God's kingdom if left unattended, some of them might. Then God would have to attend them. Each of those further changes would have its own butterfly effect, and on and on. It is God's wisdom to know that Satan was not strong enough to unseat him, and that he should not aid Satan's cause by shaking up history with more tares[5] than Satan had already sown.

Notes

[4] "Butterfly effect," https://en.wikipedia.org/wiki/Butterfly_effect.

[5] In the KJV, the weeds in the Parable of the Weeds are referred to as *tares*. Tare is a cognate with the word *tear* wherein the night shift would have *torn up* history with their evil changes.

5. The Trinity

In this section, we will separate God from the Holy Spirit
and Jesus. This is the nature of the trinity: God as
a younger man fighting for victory, God himself having
attained absolute dominion, and God's intention: three
parts of a whole. In the preceding sections, we have made
the point to put God in the seat at timelike infinity, but
now we will seat the Holy Spirit there to assign God as
a human man. Jesus is God as a younger man before he
completes the mission of the Messiah. God is Jesus as an
older man after the harvest has come and he has affected
the final defeat of Satan in some present moment. This
defeat should take the form of the collection and burning
of Satan's weeds, or tares, followed by the gathering of
the good seed.

Among all the changes enacted by all the agents, and
after all the generations of mankind have come and gone,
whose intention for what history ought to have been will
dominate at infinity? We propose that the intentions
of the man God are those which survive until the end.
For this reason, the Holy Spirit is called by God's name.
When all was said and done, it was his intention which
survived to infinity. As the winner of the time travel war,
God is the greatest and winningest warrior of all time.

Genesis 6:1-2 (KJV)

15

> 1 And it came to pass, when men began to multiply on the face of the earth, and daughters were born unto them, 2 That the sons of God saw the daughters of men that they were fair; and they took them wives of all which they chose.

Jesus is often said to be God's only son which contradicts the account of God given in Genesis 6. Genesis contains material which Jesus knew well enough to answer the Pharisees in all of their challenges.[6] The law is contained in other books as well: the rest of the books of Moses, the histories, the prophets, etc. However, Genesis is the primary account of the Lord. Genesis 6 records that God had multiple sons, not just one, and it is implied that they bred with human women. It does not say if they married them in the future or in the past, but only humans can breed with humans. The father of a human is also a human. God is a human man with multiple sons. Jesus is referred to as God's only son because he is God's only *self* as a younger man. On many such occasions, the Bible makes it clear that God is a man.

Exodus 15:3 (KJV)

3 The Lord is a man of war: the Lord is his name.

The Lord is a man. For this reason, we complete the

16

trinity with the Holy Spirit being an ephemeral orchestrator that conducts the universe from timelike infinity. As stated, the Holy Spirit is also called God because it is the intention of the man God that survives until the end. These were the stakes of the time travel war. God was the winner. In the position at the end of time, all knowledge is funneled into the omniscient Holy Spirit. We also give a mechanism explaining why God asks such questions as, "Where have you been?,"[7] and, "Who told you that you were naked?"[8] The man God is not omniscient. Anything is possible for God because the Holy Spirit can write any course of history. There is no one at a time later than infinity who might overwrite God's changes. The Holy Spirit is omnipotent, but God Almighty is almighty in the sense of being very mighty, not in the sense of being omnipotent. No man is omnipotent, but the power that makes the final decisions at the end is exactly that, and it supports God.

Before the Israelites entered the Promised Land, for 38 years the Lord's hand was against the generation of fighting men that had fled Egypt with Moses.[9] In the magical sense of omnipotence, one wonders why God would put his hand against them for almost 40 years when he could have snapped his fingers against them in a moment. In the time travel interpretation, the 38 years may well have been mere moments from God's point of view as he shepherded them across the wilderness where he would stop in by time travel to guide, teach, and chastise them only every so often. When God is a man, we see that he must do work to eliminate the generation of fighting men from Egypt by putting his hand against them. The idea of God as a human man will be one of the most foreign ideas to many believers, so we will continue to motivate the idea throughout the remainder of this study. Presently, we suggest that what most people call God is really the Holy Spirit. God himself is a mighty warrior and a great king[10] in the form of a human man.

Genesis 49:10 (NIV)

10 The scepter will not depart from Judah,
   nor the ruler's staff from between his feet,
until he to whom it belongs shall come
   and the obedience of the nations shall be
   his.

When Jacob told the fortunes of his children from his deathbed in Genesis 49, the first Biblical mention of the Messiah is given. In the NIV, the footnote to "he to whom it belongs" is, "Or *to whom tribute belongs*; the meaning of the Hebrew for this phrase is uncertain." We will take this person to be the man God himself. In Section 12, we will point out some problems related to Jacob's fortune telling, but we will accept his proclamation that someone is coming who is the owner of the ruler's staff. This is corroborated many times as a central theme in the Bible's telling of glory to come.

THE TIME TRAVEL INTERPRETATION OF THE BIBLE

> ## Revelation 1:8 (KJV)
>
> 8 I am Alpha and Omega, the beginning and the ending, saith the Lord, which is, and which was, and which is to come, the Almighty.

Revelation 1 gives a direct chronological sense of the trinity, but it may speak more to the existence of God at multiple times due to his tradecraft in time travel. While the reference to simultaneous existences in the past, present, and future is intuitive, it may be remarked upon that the future-directed condition is that God "is to come" as opposed to *will always be*. When God is to come, we may extrapolate the eventual birth of the man God at some point in the future relative to the time of John of Patmos, the author of Revelation.

> ## Zechariah 14:9 (NIV)
>
> 9 The Lord will be king over the whole earth. On that day there will be one Lord, and his name the only name.

> ## Isaiah 66:23-24 (NIV)

> **23** ["]From one New Moon to another and from one Sabbath to another, all mankind will come and bow down before me," says the Lord. **24** "And they will go out and look on the dead bodies of those who rebelled against me; the worms that eat them will not die, the fire that burns them will not be quenched, and they will be loathsome to all mankind."

God is described many times as a celestial king reigning on high from heaven, but God is also described as an earthly king. We associate this latter kingship with the coming of the Kingdom of God at which time the person of Jesus should give way to the person of God. At that time, the son will become the father. This joint person is the one Jacob refers to in Genesis 49 as "he to whom it belongs." He is Almighty God. It all belongs to God, and there is no other reasonable conclusion for the identity of the person to whom it might belong. One day, the man God will be king over the whole Earth. This is the mission of the Messiah: to conquer the world and command the obedience of the nations.

In the New Testament, Jesus does not command the obedience of the Israelites, the Romans, or any other nation, but a second coming is told in which such things will take place. For the reason that Jesus did not command the obedience of the nations, and for other reasons, we will attach some nuance to the person of Jesus in Section 18.

Notes

[6]E.g.: Luke 2:41-47, etc.
[7]Job 1:7.
[8]Genesis 3:11.
[9]Deuteronomy 2:14-15.
[10]Psalm 24:8.

6. God the Creator

The Lord is a man of war.[11] He is also a man of creation. The creation of the universe follows after God's victory in the time travel war. If God gets to write history, then he gets to write it all the way from the beginning. In this section, we will explore and suggest the idea that God himself, the man God, created the first time machine. Due to the grandfather paradox, whoever created the first time machine would be invincible up until the point where that work was done. The ancestors of that person could never be exterminated to prevent his existence because then the time machine which allowed someone to kill them would never be invented. While it is impossible to say what would have happened in an earlier time travel war before creation, it is reasonable to assume that God would write the current arc of history to be such that he himself is the one who benefits from the invincible status of the original creator of time travel. God may have been that man all along giving him a foundation of strength in the time before creation. Since this invincibility would expire at the time when the work was done, one assumes that many battles in the time travel war were fought by those who wanted to kill God to take his place on the path to timelike infinity. Indeed, Satan's rebellion is described as an attempt to establish his own throne above God's.[12]

In Section 18, we will frame Jesus' death and resurrection in terms of a successful attempt to kill God. The attempt's subsequent timeline ultimately failed to reach infinity where God was able to rewrite his earlier timeline from death onto life. The current *Anno Domini* age of the Earth, meaning *Years of Dominion* or *Years of our Lord*, will refer to the establishment of God's earthly dominion by his demonstration that even killing his younger self is not sufficient to unseat him from his throne of eternal glory and unlimited power. Those who kill God eventually die, and their intentions never make it until the end. History is rewritten, and the Lord is resurrected. Then their intention is gone and God remains.

Psalm 104:5 (NIV)

5   He set the earth on its foundations;
    it can never be moved.

In the context of the past, present, and future, Psalm 104 relates that God set the present on the past. In the context of God the Creator, the immovability of the earth speaks to a grandfather paradox ensuring that God's creation can never be disrupted. God set all of history on its foundations. He created the time machine at a time before he would go on to create the entire universe from his seat of ultimate victory.

From the end, God made the beginning. The work of ages is to draw a line that connects the two. In this way, we see a system of reason in God allowing wickedness into creation. As the first timeline grew toward the future, God intended good things. Satan appeared in the Garden of Eden to give Adam and Eve some knowledge that became a problem. Rather than starting over, God worked around Satan. Now the seed of God's good timeline grows toward the time of the harvest whereupon God's kingdom will be established. In the meantime, God has chosen to work around the wicked things people wrote into history rather than to uproot all of it. God's part was to allow the weeds to grow, but it was not God that planted them. Unbelievers blame God for the existence of the weeds, but the true telling is more complicated than that. God did not plant the weeds but it will be God that burns them at the end.

Isaiah 45:7 (KJV)

7 I form the light, and create darkness: I make peace, and create evil: I the Lord do all these things.

In Isaiah 45, there is no need to read to more into this than that God nurtures those who keep his covenants and destroys those who don't. However, it is also possible to understand that by creating the time machine, God indirectly created the evil that was done with it. Since we have put forth the notion that God's work is to connect a timeline from creation to the establishment of a kingdom from which his good intentions will go on forever, the evil timelines that spring up along the way may be attributed to God's creation as well.

Notes

[11]Exodus 15:3.
[12]Isaiah 14:13-14.

7. False Gods

During the kingdoms of Israel and Judah, and earlier and later, false gods were a big problem for the Lord. The history summarized in Section 15 shows that the Israelites would serve false gods not known to their ancestors at every seeming opportunity.[13] Sometimes false gods are described as mere idols of wood and stone. Sometimes they are described as more than that. In this section, we will describe the latter sort as other time travelers.

Leviticus 20:1-5 (NIV)

1 The Lord said to Moses, 2 "Say to the Israelites: 'Any Israelite or any foreigner residing in Israel who sacrifices any of his children to Molek is to be put to death. The members of the community are to stone him. 3 I myself will set my face against him and will cut him off from his people; for by sacrificing his children to Molek, he has defiled my sanctuary and profaned my holy name. 4 If the members of the community close their eyes when that man sacrifices one of his children to Molek and if they fail to put him to death, 5 I myself will set my face against him and his family and will cut them off from their people together with all who follow him in prostituting themselves to Molek.[']"]

By commanding earlier people to kill their children, false gods were able to prevent the existence of certain people in the future. Without a doubt, many tried to kill God in this way. They may or may not have understood that the man God was protected from such things by the grandfather paradox. They would think, "If God can get to timelike infinity, then I can do it too and replace him." A problem in this thinking on the part of the false gods is that there is no good reason to think that God replaced anyone in his own ascension. More likely, God was the only one to make it all the way until the end. Questions about what came before creation will beg any number of further questions, but, in the opinion of this writer, it would be impossible to unseat someone who already had the high ground at timelike infinity. In this way, there is no god but God.

Psalm 95:3-5 (NIV)

3   For the Lord is the great God,
        the great King above all gods.
4   In his hand are the depths of the earth,
        and the mountain peaks belong to him.
5   The sea is his, for he made it,
        and his hands formed the dry land.

God being above the other gods, the false gods, is a condition given by the ultimate failure of all of God's contenders. The word for *god* should be understood to be God's name and not the name of one of God's adversaries for the same reason. An association with the word *god* makes an appeal to a special place for the English language, but if God the Creator was writing scientific papers in the post-Einsteinian era, those papers would almost certainly have been written in English, barring some great change in the structure of the scientific establishment.

Isaiah 43:9-13 (NIV)

9   All the nations gather together
        and the peoples assemble.
    Which of their gods foretold this
        and proclaimed to us the former things?
    Let them bring in their witnesses to prove
    they were right,
        so that others may hear and say, "It is
        true."
10 "You are my witnesses," declares the Lord,
        "and my servant whom I have chosen,
    so that you may know and believe me
        and understand that I am he.
    Before me no god was formed,
        nor will there be one after me.
11 I, even I, am the Lord,
        and apart from me there is no savior.

> 12   I have revealed and saved and proclaimed—
>   I, and not some foreign god among you.
>   You are my witnesses," declares the Lord,
>   "that I am God.
> 13   Yes, and from ancient days I am he.
>   No one can deliver out of my hand.
>   When I act, who can reverse it?"

In Isaiah 43, God compares himself to other gods which we view as other time travelers vying against him in the battle for control over eternity. God proves his mastery in verse nine by asking, "Who foretold the true course of events?" As such, the timelines of the false gods necessarily diverge from God's true timeline when the falsehood of their prophecy is revealed. God's timeline is the true vine that starts with creation and reaches eternity through the coming of the Messiah. Along the way, God can always alter the false gods' timelines to send them away into destruction. When God sets a timeline, there is no one at any later time who might reverse it.

Notes

[13]E.g.: Exodus 32:2-4, 1 Kings 12:28-30, Psalm 106:37-38, Jeremiah 7:31, Ezekiel 16:20-21, etc.

8. Creation Through the Flood

If every instance of *the earth* in the Bible and every instance of *the sea* were to be read as *the present* and *the past* respectively, then that would mean that the earth and the sea have no direct mentions in the Bible. This is unlikely. One must keep in mind that the Old Testament—essentially the Hebrew Bible including the Torah, the histories, and the major and minor prophets—was written in an ancient language having not nearly the number of words found in modern languages. Modern languages still have words with multiple meanings, and the occurrence of such words in the original scripture would have been amplified due to the limited contextual lexicon. Beyond the ambiguity related to such homonyms, the idiom of the culture using the words was lost long before any of it was translated into ancient Greek. Thus, there is a high degree of flexibility induced when the text is rendered in modern languages such as English. For this reason and others, it can depend on nothing more than one's discretion to read an instance of *the earth* as referring to the present or to the land or soil.

Genesis 1:1-2 (NIV)

1 In the beginning God created the heavens and the earth. 2 Now the earth was formless

> and empty, darkness was over the surface
> of the deep, and the Spirit of God was
> hovering over the waters.

In the Bible's first verses, the past, present, and future are identified. By the second verse, we have distinguished between God himself and the Spirit of God which we have previously called the Holy Spirit. Genesis 1 is usually taken to refer to God's creation of the universe and not only the planet Earth. In the usual way, the Earth is our planet, or the earth is the soil that we tread upon, and the heavens are the rest of the universe. In the time travel interpretation, verse one says that God created the present and the future. Under the context of God as the creator of all things including time travel, it follows that God would have created the future and the present before he could create the past. At some point in the work of the man God, he would have had an idea for some new principle. In the future relative to that time, the first time machine was built. Only at times later than that would God have had access to the past. Even then, the Spirit of God was already hovering over *the waters* because all times exist simultaneously in the 4D view of spacetime. Timelike infinity is later than any finite time in the 3D view, but it is simply the ceiling things in 4D. There is no future relative to timelike infinity, so all of time is in the past with respect to the Spirit of God. For this reason, the Spirit of God hovers above *the waters*, as in verse 2.

31

> ## Genesis 1:3-5 (NIV)
>
> 3 And God said, "Let there be light," and there
> was light. 4 God saw that the light was good,
> and he separated the light from the darkness
> 5 God called the light "day," and the dark-
> ness he called "night." And there was even-
> ing, and there was morning—the first day.

From the end of time, God said, "Let there be light."
Light was good, and this was the good seed that God
planted. After God won the right to write history, he
said, "Let there be a good creation," and he separated
good from evil. In the idiom of time travel, the "day"
shift represents the force of good in creation, and the
"night" shift represents the force of wickedness. Although
God planted good seed, weeds would soon be planted in
Genesis 3.

God created the present and the future, and then the
past. As the winner of the war over who would be the
author of history, from timelike infinity God created the
beginning of time, the earliest moment, and this begs a
well known question about what came before the beginning. Once the original time travel war was over, the
one in which God first ascended to infinity, the linear
flow of time was restored without who knows what kind
of problems that would have arisen during a war fought
with time machines. Although God would have created

the earliest time in the sense of chronologically laminar time, there would exist a past that was earlier than the earliest moment of God's creation: the past on an unbroken worldline of God's own *proper time*.[14] This follows from the idea that God arrived at timelike infinity before the creation of the universe. Namely, God must have had some earlier history before he could have arrived at the beginning.

Here, we will not answer the question about how it all started to begin with. Perhaps time has a circular topology in which questions about an absolute beginning are not well defined. The Spirit of God is above the mind of man, and certain mysteries may be unknowable.

Genesis 1:6-8 (NIV)

6 And God said, "Let there be a vault between the waters to separate water from water." 7 So God made the vault and separated the water under the vault from the water above it. And it was so. 8 God called the vault "sky." And there was evening, and there was morning—the second day.

This is what it means for God to separate water from water: God separated the chronology of the new creation under his throne in *the sky* from the past that preceded his ultimate victory. In the sense of Einsteinian relativity, all timelines must converge to timelike infinity. Once time travel weapons are introduced, however, it becomes possible that information about certain past histories can be lost or destroyed. The physics of such a mechanism is complicated, and the reader is asked to take if for granted that God was able to cast the earlier history out into the darkness beyond the vault of the sky. More details regarding such things are given in Section 17.

Genesis 1:26 (NIV)

26 Then God said, "Let us make mankind in our image, in our likeness, so that they may rule over the fish in the sea and the birds in the sky, over the livestock and all the wild animals, and over all the creatures that move along the ground."

This is the first of a few Biblical instances wherein God refers to some *us* which is not well understood in canonical theology. To make sense of it, we must understand the context of the time travel war. If history is the limit of an infinite number of revisions, not all of the revisions favoring God's intention would have been enacted by the man God himself. In a familiar way, the fighting would have spurred the formation of factions. It is our thesis that God's victory comes in part from his good intentions being favored on long timescales by those factions that would have their children live in such good conditions. It follows that the cumulative effect of many changes over long timescales is preferential toward God's intention. God wins the time travel war because the future that unfolds following the establishment of his kingdom is the best future. It is superior to the future created by each and every contender. In this way, the Spirit of God remains at the end of time, not the spirit of any of God's enemies.

Now we have generated a context for the mysterious *us* to whom God refers at the end of Genesis 1. Those in fellowship with God would be those fighting for God such as Michael and his angels who we will discuss in the next section. Such persons would be time travelers from God's future and those who fought for God in God's present: God's agents.

The second chapter of Genesis gives a first hint of the complex and/or nonlinear chronology of the telling of things in the Bible.[15] In Genesis 1, we learned that God created plants on the third day, and that he did not create people until the sixth day.[16] However, the second chapter's context regards events after God had created Adam but before any plants had started to grow. The narrative advances to the time when God had planted the Garden of Eden, and we learn about the Tree of Life and the Tree of the Knowledge of Good and Evil.[17] Although we did not get the context in Genesis 1, further reading in Genesis 2 reveals that the actual course of events was that God created plants, created man, then waited for plants to spring up, and then created woman afterwards;

the chronology of the events was complicated. Throughout the remainder of this study, we will sometimes make
the case that God is speaking from his own time in a
different order than his words are recorded in the Bible.
For instance, we will make the case that God is likely to
have spoken to Isaiah from a later time in his own life
than he spoke to Jeremiah and Ezekiel though they were
prophets after Isaiah. This sort of context is well motivated by the complex chronology presented in the second
chapter of Genesis.

The serpent appears in the third chapter of Genesis.[18]
To understand a talking serpent, the reader is forced to
believe in what is tantamount to magic, not to believe the
Bible at all, or to search for an alternative interpretation.
Serpents can't speak. They don't have vocal chords. It
is true that God will curse the serpent to slither on the
ground and eat dust, but here we will understand that
the serpent is the man Satan appearing in the very early
history by time travel. God's curse on the serpent was
as follows.

Genesis 3:14-15 (NIV)

14 So the Lord God said to the serpent, "Because
you have done this,

> "Cursed are you above all livestock
>   and all wild animals!

> You will crawl on your belly
>   and you will eat dust
>   all the days of your life.
> 15 "And I will put enmity
>   between you and the woman,
>   and between your offspring and hers;
>   he will crush your head,
>   and you will strike his heel."

What was God's curse on Satan after he poisoned Adam through his wife Eve? It is difficult to know. We will return to this curse after we discuss God's covenant with Noah near the end of this section and again in the next section. What was the nature of the poison in the fruit? One may speculate to any ends. To the extent that the forbidden fruit came from the Tree of the Knowledge of Good and Evil—knowledge of the light and the dark that the Lord had separated—it may be that Satan showed Eve what things were like in the war before creation. Then Eve showed Adam. Then they lost their innocence by the knowledge of such evil. God's good creation was poisoned. For this interpretation, the concept of a tree in the middle of the Garden is well suited to a complex of divergent worldlines at the point where God separated the waters.

As God's curse on the serpent goes on, it is clear that the pronouns are not definitely identified. One may assume that the *he* in verse 15 is Adam, but the rest of Adam's life is chronicled in Genesis, and crushing a head

37

is never mentioned. An alternative, arguably better interpretation is as follows. In the future, one of Eve's descendants will crush Satan's head. Perhaps the figurative head of the descendants of Satan will be crushed. Overall, an enmity cited between the respective descendants of Adam and Eve and Satan speaks somewhat to the Parable of the Weeds in which God has left the final reckoning until the end of the age. Furthermore, although Abraham's grandson Jacob, who we will presume to be Satan,[19] was himself a descendant of Eve, we may differentiate Satan's offspring in his own time, the Israelites who are God's ancestors, from the offspring Satan might have had in his own distant past. These early people would have been planted by Satan in furtherance of his intention to undermine God by creating a lineage of people believing that he, and not the Lord, is the master of all things. Going back in time to create a lineage of people having a given future person as their god would have been tried many times in the time travel war. God himself does this. Unlike the other gods, God is not a false god. The Spirit of God is seated at infinity and not the spirit of any of God's enemies. It is God's spirit that survives until the end. This is the main difference between God and his rivals: the false Gods. Satan is a particular case because he is from God's own ancestral lineage.

God's curse on Adam was such that he would have to work the land to live rather than to live in the Garden's plentiful abundance.[20] On the land, Adam's firstborn son Cain took to agriculture. His second son Abel took to shepherding.[21] When Cain and Abel brought their offerings to the Lord, God preferred Abel's. Then Cain killed Abel in his jealousy.[22] God's curse on Cain was a furtherance of his curse on Adam: after Abel's murder, Cain's work on the soil would no longer bear fruit. He was forced to wander the Earth.[23] Cain protested to the Lord complaining that anyone who might find him wandering would kill him.[24] Who would those other people have been to find and kill him? They would have been the weeds planted by Satan and/or the false gods. Although God had already separated *the waters under the sky* from *the other waters*, the presence of these other people beyond the Garden suggests that certain parties may have transited from one body of water into the other before God created his vault on the second day.

Genesis 5:28-29 (KJV)

28 And Lamech lived an hundred eighty and two years, and begat a son: 29 And he called his name Noah, saying, This same shall comfort us concerning our work and toil of our hands, because of the ground which the Lord hath cursed.

Adam lived to be 930 years old, at least 800 of which were spent outside of the Garden. Many subsequent generations came and went. Then Noah was born. The reiteration of God's curse on Adam by Noah's father in

Genesis 5 gives the curse an acute and bitter connotation. More than 1,000 years have passed, and God's curse of the forbidden fruit has been on the people all along. The Parable of the Weeds, however, should lessen the apparent bitterness. The context of the curse was that God had chosen not to fix the problem caused by Satan's action in the Garden until some time in the future. We have associated this time with the period following God's birth and the completion of his good work at the time of the harvest. The curse on Adam and his descendants was that they would have to bear the consequences of Adam's sin until then. As it is written, the kingdom of heaven is like a man who sowed good seed in his field, but someone came and planted weeds in it.

The curse on Adam and his descendants is not God's cruelty. Instead, it is God's wisdom that it is better to leave Adam and early man with a curse than to engage in the time travel tit for tat of trying to prevent Satan from appearing to Eve in the first place. At the end of time, the Spirit of God determines that this course of history is the best way to build the past upon which will rest the Kingdom of God. Adam had no memory of life outside the Garden, but life in God's kingdom will be sweetened by the collective memory of the alternative.

Genesis 6:1-8 (NIV)

1 When human beings began to increase in num-

ber on the earth and daughters were born to them, 2 the sons of God saw that the daughters of humans were beautiful, and they married any of them they chose. 3 Then the Lord said, "My Spirit will not contend with humans forever, for they are mortal; their days will be a hundred and twenty years."

4 The Nephilim were on the earth in those days— and also afterward—when the sons of God went to the daughters of humans and had children by them. They were the heroes of old, men of renown.

5 The Lord saw how great the wickedness of the human race had become on the earth, and that every inclination of the thoughts of the human heart was only evil all the time. 6 The Lord regretted that he had made human beings on the earth, and his heart was deeply troubled. 7 So the Lord said, "I will wipe from the face of the earth the human race I have created—and with them the animals, the birds and the creatures that move along the ground—for I regret that I have made them." 8 But Noah found favor in the eyes of the Lord.

Genesis 6:2 may be the most ignored verse in the Bible. Jesus was not God's only son. Jesus was God's only self as a younger man. The only way to the father is through the son in the manner that the way to an older man can only be through his younger self.

God wanted humans to live in the garden that he had separated from the darkness, but that was not possible in the aftermath of the encounter with the serpent. The fruit of the Tree of the Knowledge of Good and Evil was some learning of what had come before God's creation: learning about the dark side of things. God had crafted a nice place for humans from the beginning, but, as events unfolded, mankind would have to wait for the coming of the Kingdom of God to live the toil-free and good life that God intended. Between the Garden and the Kingdom, things got very bad. God regretted making people at all, as in verse six. Regarding the earlier curse on Adam, we found that the Spirit of God must have decided that the present course was for the best. Perhaps a rebellion is inevitable among a people with free will, and it is better to have it at an early time than a late one. As it was, God nearly decided otherwise. He was going to destroy everything in the wake of the evil that had come of the rebellion. In the end, God decided to destroy everything except for Noah and his family. This is a recurring theme in the Bible. No matter the disaster that falls on God's people, there is always a remnant that survives. This unbroken line is required to preserve the continuity between the beginning of time, God's eventual birth, his subsequent invention of time travel, and then his final victory and the perpetuation of his righteous intention to the end of time.

Genesis 7:11-12 (KJV)

11 In the six hundredth year of Noah's life, in the second month, the seventeenth day of the month, the same day were all the fountains of the great deep broken up, and the windows of heaven were opened. **12** And the rain was upon the earth forty days and forty nights.

The story of the flood appears in many cultures. It is not only a story in the Bible. Even the indigenous Hawaiians have a story about Nu'u and a great flood, as do many other cultures. As it was with the talking serpent, the story of the flood is semi-magical, and we will remove the magical character of the events by invoking the time travel interpretation. In that case, God let loose the full disorder of time travel war to destroy all life in Noah's present except for Noah and his ark.

Genesis 7:18-19 (NIV)

18 For forty days the flood kept coming on the earth, and as the waters increased they lifted the ark high above the earth. **19** They rose greatly on the earth, and all the high mountains under the entire heavens were covered.

JONATHAN W. TOOKER

There is not enough water on Earth to cover the mountains. Rather, all the high mountains under the entire *future* must refer to all the divergent future timelines swirling about in a developing and tumultuous universe. God had established his victory timeline before the flood, but his numerous later admonishments against service to false gods are strong evidence that other timelines were present in the interim. The difference between the Sovereign Lord and the many false gods is that the false gods' intentions die out before infinity. In the present case, the Lord drown them with his flood while his own intention goes on to dominate forever following the establishment of his kingdom. We understand that *all the high mountains* under *the entire heavens* must refer to the destruction of even the most prominent competing timelines extending farthest into the future. In the sense of relativistic spacetime, the hypersurface of the present always *floats* on the sea of the past. Any surface of constant proper time is seen floating on earlier times in an elementary depiction of Minkowski space.[25] Therefore, Noah's floating on the surface of the water, which is well enough understood in relation to some mysterious volume of water, is best understood to mean that the ark was a time bubble not destroyed when the Lord rent his creation with springs from *the deep* and the floodgates of *heaven.*

God's first Biblical covenant is with Noah.[26] Throughout this study, we will always take God's covenants in relation to God's own bloodline. God's covenant with Noah was that he would not destroy him or his sons in the flood. God's genetic material would come to him beyond the flood through Noah, his sons, and their wives. When the flood receded and Noah lived on land again, the Lord promised Noah that he would never again destroy all life.

Genesis 8:20-22 (NIV)

20 Then Noah built an altar to the Lord and, taking some of all the clean animals and clean birds, he sacrificed burnt offerings on it. 21 The Lord smelled the pleasing aroma and said in his heart: "Never again will I curse the ground because of humans, even though every inclination of the human heart is evil from childhood. And never again will I destroy all living creatures, as I have done.

22 "As long as the earth endures,
seedtime and harvest,
cold and heat,
summer and winter,
day and night
will never cease."

Consider the specific form of the words God spoke in his heart in verse 22. The progression of seedtime and harvest, summer and winter, and day and night speak of God's promise to never again let loose the total destruction of time travel weapons. Each of God's examples in what will later be called God's covenant with the day and night is an example of the linear progression of the cycles of time. Even cold and heat relate to what is called the thermodynamic arrow of time.[27] Given the context, one might ask how the eternal continuation of day passing into night and night into day would relate to a flood of water. On the other hand, if this is God's promise to never again use temporal weaponry, then the context is well fitting. These are the words God spoke in his heart: "Never again will I destroy you *as I have done.* Day will pass into night and night will pass into day uninterrupted forever."

Genesis 9:1-2 (NIV)

1 Then God blessed Noah and his sons, saying to them, "Be fruitful and increase in number and fill the earth. 2 The fear and dread of you will fall on all the beasts of the earth, and on all the birds in the sky, on every creature that moves along the ground, and on all the fish in the sea; they are given into your hands."

The earlier things were destroyed. However, the false gods that are the Lord's enemies eventually came along from somewhere. Maybe these were rebels from Noah's future different from Satan only in that Satan is God's ancestor. As Satan was able to drop in on the Garden of Eden, the false gods were still working to seed their own people alongside Noah, his sons, and their wives. So, one wonders about the beasts that will dread Noah and his descendants, as in verse two. Who were they? When God resolved to let loose the flood in Genesis 6, he would kill the human race *that he had created* as well as all the other animals. Accordingly, we suggest that the bloodlines spawned by God's enemies are lumped in with *the beasts*. After the flood, God would ensure that the members of his enemies' bloodlines would dread Noah and his descendants.

Now we have an acute context for Satan's villainy. He and his people were not mere beasts but were instead humans from God's own lineage. Furthermore, we have a context for God's curse on the serpent following the encounter in the garden. God told the serpent, "Cursed are you above all livestock and all wild animals!"[28] In this way, if God is referring to the descendants of the false gods as wild animals, then God's curse is that Satan should be even more damned than are those other people: the beasts. To the extent that it is not fitting with the present interpretation that God might have turned Satan into a snake, a ready interpretation for the remainder of God's curse on the serpent is given in the following section.

Notes

[14]Proper time is the time on a clock carried with a particular individual. Should an individual use a time machine to travel to an earlier time, the time on his wristwatch will show that the earlier time is later in his own *proper time*. For example, proper time measures the time in which one does not become younger by traveling to the past. "Proper time," https://en.wikipedia.org/wiki/Proper_time.

[15]Genesis 2:4-5.

[16]Genesis 1:11-27.

[17]Genesis 2:8-9.

[18]Genesis 3:1.

[19]This notion is developed most specifically in Sections 11, 12, 13, and 14.

[20]Genesis 3:17-19.

[21]Genesis 4:2.

[22]Genesis 4:8.

[23]Genesis 4:12.

[24]Genesis 4:14.

[25]"Minkowski space: Causal structure," https://en.wikipedia.org/wiki/Minkowski_space.

[26]Genesis 6:17-18.

[27]"Arrow of time: Thermodynamic arrow of time," https://en.wikipedia.org/wiki/Arrow_of_time.

[28]Genesis 3:14.

9. The Time Travel War

In this section, we will discuss the time travel war waged by Satan, descendant of Adam, against God, descendant of Satan and creator of Adam. This section does not pertain to the war which would have preceded the account of creation given in Genesis.

Revelation 12:7-10 (NIV)

7 Then war broke out in heaven. Michael and his angels fought against the dragon, and the dragon and his angels fought back. 8 But he was not strong enough, and they lost their place in heaven. 9 The great dragon was hurled down—that ancient serpent called the devil, or Satan, who leads the whole world astray. He was hurled to the earth, and his angels with him.

10 Then I heard a loud voice in heaven say:

> "Now have come the salvation and the power
> and the kingdom of our God,
> and the authority of his Messiah.
> For the accuser of our brothers and sisters,
> who accuses them before our God day and
> night,
> has been hurled down.

The context in Revelation 12 is that an angel, or an *agent*, revealed to John of Patmos that which was to come. A war was fought in the future. Although God was not yet born at the time of John's revelation, the angel showed him God's triumph over Satan. Michael and his agents were foremost among those fighting to preserve the Lord's intention when they fought against the serpent and his agents. In the end, the serpent's renegade time team was not strong enough, and they lost their place in the future. This is to say, more or less, that their key cards got deactivated, and they could no longer fight against God with access to their respective consoles on the night shift. They were hurled down to the present, likely their times of origin, and locked out of time travel. Many of them were probably killed too.

Despite Satan's prominent position in Christian theology, he has only a few Biblical mentions between the appearance in the Garden and when he is cast out of heaven in Revelation. Sections 13 and 20 will treat the issue of Satan's direct mentions in further detail. At this point, it is commented that Satan appears on almost every page of the Bible when one understands that Israel is Satan. In that case, the chronicle in the Bible mostly tells the interactions between God and the children of Satan, called the Israelites. In Revelation 12, Satan is described as "him who leads the world astray." This refers at least to the original encounter with Eve, which preceded the curse that fell on Adam, which was compounded upon Cain, and under which very many generations of humans suffered and continue to suffer to this day. Verse ten says, "Now has come the salvation." Salvation means deliverance from harm, so it should follow that the curse on Adam is lifted upon the coming of the Kingdom of God. The authority of the Messiah refers to the authority of the third part of the trinity: God as a younger man. At the onset of the Kingdom of God, God's age is such that he is not yet God the father. Later, he will become the father when his kingdom is well established. God's enemy in this verse is referred to as "the accuser." An interpretation should be that the rebels accused God of having created the problems for which God's enemies were ultimately responsible. Then the rebels who would seek to lay blame on God for all evils were cast out. The Parable of the Weeds shows that God's part was only to find it wiser to let the weeds grow lest the good seed be ripped up with them.

Revelation 22:1-3 (NIV)

1 Then the angel showed me the river of the water of life, as clear as crystal, flowing from the throne of God and of the Lamb 2 down the middle of the great street of the city. On each side of the river stood the tree of life, bearing twelve crops of fruit, yielding its fruit every month. And the leaves of the tree are for the healing of the nations. 3 No longer will there be any curse. The throne of God and of the Lamb will be in

the city, and his servants will serve him.

It is assumed that the coming of the Kingdom of God will mark the end of the curse on Adam that mankind's lot would be a life of toil, as in verse three. God's victory in Satan's defeat will restore his intended good creation. To that end, it must be stated that certain technical nuance in physics intimately links time travel with anti-gravity and free energy. If these technologies are available in the Kingdom of God, then we will obtain a non-magical mechanism by which there shall be no toil in heaven. Adam had to work the land by the sweat of his brow, but if free-energy, anti-gravity tractors are available in the future, then the work of food production will no longer be a toilsome endeavor. Even with regards to modern food production, the endeavor will no longer be expensive. In this way, the splendor of the kingdom which is in *heaven* relative to the present time shall come in the form of a just government over which the Sovereign Lord is king, and a rich economy of abundance in which the struggle for limited resources is no longer a prominent feature.

Revelation 12:11-12 (NIV)

11 They triumphed over him
      by the blood of the Lamb

> and by the word of their testimony;
> they did not love their lives so much
> as to shrink from death.
> 12 Therefore rejoice, you heavens
> and you who dwell in them!
> But woe to the earth and the sea,
> because the devil has gone down to you!
> He is filled with fury,
> because he knows that his time is short."

The blood of the Lamb is the blood of God's Messiah: God as a younger man. Likely God himself was among them who did not love his life so much as to shrink from death in the fight against evil. The story of death and resurrection is integral to the trinity, and we will say more about that in Section 18. The war was won, and John heard the voice say, "Rejoice, you heavens and you who dwell in them! But woe to the earth and the sea because the devil has gone down to you." Those in the future will exist in the Kingdom of God, but woe to those in the past and presumably John's present because the devil has been sent there. Again, this references the past as a sour place due to the weeds planted by the devil before he was cast out by God's agents.

In the context of Satan's having been cast out of heaven, now we will interpret God's curse on the serpent: "You will crawl on your belly, and you will eat dust all the days of your life."[29] To the extent that we may associate crawling on one's belly with slithering on *the ground* (the present), Satan lost his access to times other than his own. He was cursed to live the remainder of his days as a Bronze Age man. Leaving him behind, God said, "Eat my dust, Satan." Israel tried to get ahead in his rebellion, but he would spend the rest of his days in the trailing position.

Notes

[29] Genesis 3:14.

10. The Tower of Babel

The events in Genesis 11 follow after Noah and the flood.

Genesis 11:1-9 (NIV)

1 Now the whole world had one language and a common speech. 2 As people moved eastward, they found a plain in Shinar and settled there.

3 They said to each other, "Come, let's make bricks and bake them thoroughly." They used brick instead of stone, and tar for mortar. 4 Then they said, "Come, let us build ourselves a city, with a tower that reaches to the heavens, so that we may make a name for ourselves; otherwise we will be scattered over the face of the whole earth."

5 But the Lord came down to see the city and the tower the people were building. 6 The Lord said, "If as one people speaking the same language they have begun to do this, then nothing they plan to do will be impossible for them. 7 Come, let us go down and confuse their language so they will not understand each other."

8 So the Lord scattered them from there over all the earth, and they stopped building the city. 9 That is why it was called Babel—because there

> the Lord confused the language of the whole world. From there the Lord scattered them over the face of the whole earth.

We assume that the city mentioned in verse four is either Babylon or a precursor settlement of those who would go on to found Babylon after God forbade the completion of their Tower, which was certainly a rebel time machine. Verse four relates that the people in Shinar wanted to build a time machine that would reach into *the future* so that they might make a name for themselves. The Lord saw their intention and said, "If they build their own rebel time machine, then they will be able to do whatever they seek to do." In this way, there is a context for time machines apart from the central time travel organization. It is obvious how having their own separate branch of chronology with their own time travel operation would afford them the ability to do whatever they wanted to do.

How did God confound the language? Likely God used his own time machine to go into the pasts of the people trying to build the tower, and there he altered the roots of their speech. By the time they arrived in Shinar, they could not understand each other and could not be as one people. From there, the Lord scattered them. Maybe Babel was Babylon or maybe Babylon was constructed by a remnant from Babel that still had the intention to fight against God. The thorn in the side of the Lord that was Babylon reeks of the intention to undermine the Lord on behalf of those whom the Lord undermined at Babel. We have no direct connection between Babel and Babylon other than the similarity of the names, but it seems reasonable enough to consider that Babylon may have been named in homage to the attempt to undermine the Lord in Shinar.

In support of the idea that God retroactively confounded the language using time travel, take note of Genesis 10's prior account of the splitting up of the languages of the tribes of Noah's descendants.[30] Since God had destroyed all living things not long before, the people who might have built the city in Shinar could have been none other than Noah's descendants or possibly the beasts about which we speculated as the spawn of God's enemies. Since Genesis 11 refers to people and not beasts, and since the languages of Noah's descendants were split up in the preceding chapter, it is likely that the Tower of Babel was a work of the descendants of Noah. Noah's grandsons Egypt and Canaan[31] are portrayed negatively elsewhere in the Bible, so there is no contradiction assuming a conflict between God and certain people among Noah's descendants.

Notes

[30]Genesis 10:5, Genesis 10:20, Genesis 10:31.

[31]In Genesis 10:6, the NIV records Egypt as the son of Ham son of Noah. Canaan is recorded as Egypt's brother. The KJV gives Egypt's name as Mizraim.

11. Abraham, Isaac, and Jacob

The main point of this section is to compare and contrast Abraham with his grandson Jacob before we make the case in the following sections that Jacob is Satan.

Abraham was descended from Noah through his son Shem,[32] the namesake of the Semites. Abraham was probably called a Hebrew[33] by way of his descent through Shem's great-grandson Eber.[34] Although Shem lived after the flood before which God had determined that mankind should live about 120 years,[35] Shem lived to be 500.[36] Many of his descendants achieved more than 120 years, and this is another place where we might distinguish between traditional and non-traditional interpretations for the information in the Bible. Firstly, it is not so unreasonable that early genetic material was of a higher quality, having less entropy in the telomeres or some such thing, and that early men did live for hundreds of years. This is possible, but, even then, the exterior wear and tear of the years aside from the internal creep of entropy makes it difficult to envision a multi-centenarian man doing hard labor. Then again, time travel gives an explanation in the direct sense. A man might die centuries after his birth by traveling into the future. The twins paradox[37] provides another mechanism by which early people's ages might have become exceedingly high. Depending on the particular physics of time travel, traveling through time may have such relativistic time dilation effects associated with it, ones beyond the direct method of skipping over the years.

When Abraham was 75 and while his name was still Abram, God told him to go out of his own land into another land. There, God promised to make a great nation of him.[38] At the time of God's command, Abraham was very wealthy[39] and hardly living under the curse of original sin. His was not a hard life working the soil. Once Abraham was in the new land, God told him what would happen in the future.[40] This was God's first promise that Abraham's descendants would inherit the Promised Land. He also told Abraham that his descendants would become very numerous. Since he was old, Abraham later asked God about his lack of children, and God reassured him that his descendants would become more numerous than the stars.[41] After that, Abraham's first son Ishmael was born.[42] His mother was Hagar. Then God explained that his covenant would be fulfilled through Abraham's second son Isaac whose mother was Sarah.[43]

Genesis 18:20-21 (KJV)

20 And the Lord said, Because the cry of Sodom and Gomorrah is great, and because their sin is very grievous; 21 I will go down now, and see whether they have done altogether according to the cry of it, which is come unto me; and if not, I will know.

The events in Sodom and Gomorrah transpired after

God's promise regarding Isaac but before Isaac's birth. If God was omniscient in the sense of a magical ability to know all things, there would have been no need for him to go down to Sodom and Gomorrah to verify whether or not the evil things he had heard were true, as in verse 21. Genesis 18 gives more evidence that the Lord is a human man, not an ethereal entity. Abraham's subsequent pleading with the Lord regarding the fate of Sodom also shows God in a human light.[44] God eventually agreed to spare the city if ten righteous men could be found there. As events would unfold, it was clear that God was correct in his intention to destroy the city without consideration for sparing any residents merely living within the city's wickedness but possibly not partaking in it. Even Abraham's cousin Lot who was rescued from Sodom by God's agents would go on to become the father of the Moabites and the Ammonites whose men were cursed by the Lord.[45] Since King David's great-grandmother Ruth was a Moabite and David was the ancestor of Jesus Christ,[46] we cannot say that it would have been better to destroy Sodom along with Lot and his family. Still, the overall system of events surrounding the destruction of Sodom and Gomorrah motivates God's modus operadi to destroy entire cities without separating among the people who dwell in them. As it is written: God sent his *angels*, the Sodomites tried to rape them, then the angels rescued Lot and his family, but a curse fell on Lot's male descendants anyway because his family followed in the Sodomite tradition when his daughters became pregnant by their father.[47]

Genesis 22:1-2 (NIV)

1 Some time later God tested Abraham. He said to him, "Abraham!"

"Here I am," he replied.

2 Then God said, "Take your son, your only son, whom you love—Isaac—and go to the region of Moriah. Sacrifice him there as a burnt offering on a mountain I will show you."

Some years after Isaac was born and Ismael was sent away,[48] one of the most unusual accounts of God is given. God ordered Abraham to kill Isaac. In the present interpretation, God tested more than Abraham's obedience. The Lord would have tested whether or not there was a workaround by which his kingdom might endure if Satan's rebellion was prevented by putting Satan's father to death as a child.

Genesis 17:19 (KJV)

19 And God said, Sarah thy wife shall bear thee a son indeed; and thou shalt call his name Isaac: and I will establish my covenant with him for an everlasting covenant, and with his seed after him.

Before testing Abraham, God had already promised that Isaac would have children of his own.[49] One wonders if God spoke to Abraham in Genesis 17 from a later time in his own life than the time from which he had already spoken to him in Genesis 22. Abraham obeyed God and brought Isaac to the place of the sacrifice. There, it was the Lord's angel and not the Lord himself who called to Abraham telling him not to kill the boy.[50] In this way, we get a sense of complementary activities between the man God, who is called the Living God, and the Holy Spirit which is all-knowing: the Spirit of God. Perhaps the man God wanted to prevent the birth of Satan, but the omniscient Holy Spirit found that it was better to leave the problem of Satan until the end of the age. Perhaps it was God himself who changed his mind after viewing the alternative futures. In either case, God would have tested Abraham's obedience, even under the previous promise that his son would live, as well as the necessity of his own lineage through Abraham's grandson. In the end, Abraham obeyed God and did everything God required of him. The Spirit of God cemented Abraham's place in the history he has written.

The life of Isaac is given little attention, and then Isaac's twin sons are born: Esau the elder and Jacob the younger.[51]

Genesis 25:27-34 (NIV)

27 The boys grew up, and Esau became a skillful hunter, a man of the open country, while Jacob was content to stay at home among the tents. 28 Isaac, who had a taste for wild game, loved Esau, but Rebekah loved Jacob.

29 Once when Jacob was cooking some stew, Esau came in from the open country, famished. 30 He said to Jacob, "Quick, let me have some of that red stew! I'm famished!" (That is why he was also called Edom.)

31 Jacob replied, "First sell me your birthright."

32 "Look, I am about to die," Esau said. "What good is the birthright to me?"

33 But Jacob said, "Swear to me first." So he swore an oath to him, selling his birthright to Jacob.

34 Then Jacob gave Esau some bread and some lentil stew. He ate and drank, and then got up and left.

So Esau despised his birthright.

We are introduced to Jacob in Genesis 25 when he takes Esau's birthright. This account presents Jacob in a poor light. In the remainder of this section, we will make a careful character study of Jacob's excessive self-interest and lack of Abrahamic characteristics. We will show that the blessings which came to Abraham for doing what was right in God's eyes could not have come to Jacob for that reason.

> ## Genesis 26:2-5 (NIV)
>
> 2 The Lord appeared to Isaac and said, "Do not go down to Egypt; live in the land where I tell you to live. 3 Stay in this land for a while, and I will be with you and will bless you. For to you and your descendants I will give all these lands and will confirm the oath I swore to your father Abraham. 4 I will make your descendants as numerous as the stars in the sky and will give them all these lands, and through your offspring all nations on earth will be blessed, 5 because Abraham obeyed me and did everything I required of him, keeping my commands, my decrees and my instructions."

After Jacob took his brother's birthright, which was recorded strangely as being "despised" by Esau, God commanded Isaac in Genesis 26 not to go to Egypt. God reaffirmed his covenant that the Promised Land would be given to Abraham's descendants and that they would become more numerous than the stars in the sky. Unlike in previous promises, here God tells Isaac that these things will happen because Abraham found favor in the eyes of the Lord. He does not comment on Isaac in that regard.

Eventually, Isaac and his family moved to a different region in Canaan. There again, God reaffirmed that his blessing upon Isaac and his descendants was granted for Abraham's sake.[52]

Genesis 27:1-31 (KJV)

1 And it came to pass, that when Isaac was old, and his eyes were dim, so that he could not see, he called Esau his eldest son, and said unto him, My son: and he said unto him, Behold, here am I.

2 And he said, Behold now, I am old, I know not the day of my death:

3 Now therefore take, I pray thee, thy weapons, thy quiver and thy bow, and go out to the field, and take me some venison;

4 And make me savoury meat, such as I love, and bring it to me, that I may eat; that my soul may bless thee before I die.

5 And Rebekah heard when Isaac spake to Esau his son. And Esau went to the field to hunt for venison, and to bring it.

6 And Rebekah spake unto Jacob her son, saying, Behold, I heard thy father speak unto Esau thy brother, saying,

7 Bring me venison, and make me savoury meat, that I may eat, and bless thee before the Lord before my death.

8 Now therefore, my son, obey my voice according to that which I command thee.

9 Go now to the flock, and fetch me from thence two good kids of the goats; and I will make them savoury meat for thy father, such as he loveth:

10 And thou shalt bring it to thy father, that he may eat, and that he may bless thee before his death.

11 And Jacob said to Rebekah his mother, Behold, Esau my brother is a hairy man, and I am a smooth man:

12 My father peradventure will feel me, and I shall seem to him as a deceiver; and I shall bring a curse upon me, and not a blessing.

13 And his mother said unto him, Upon me be thy curse, my son: only obey my voice, and go fetch me them.

14 And he went, and fetched, and brought them to his mother: and his mother made savoury meat, such as his father loved.

15 And Rebekah took goodly raiment of her eldest son Esau, which were with her in the house, and put them upon Jacob her younger son:

16 And she put the skins of the kids of the goats upon his hands, and upon the smooth of his neck:

17 And she gave the savoury meat and the bread, which she had prepared, into the hand of her son Jacob.

18 And he came unto his father, and said, My father: and he said, Here am I; who art thou, my son?

19 And Jacob said unto his father, I am Esau thy first born; I have done according as thou badest me: arise, I pray thee, sit and eat of my venison, that thy soul may bless me.

20 And Isaac said unto his son, How is it that thou hast found it so quickly, my son? And he said, Because the Lord thy God brought it to me.

21 And Isaac said unto Jacob, Come near, I pray thee, that I may feel thee, my son, whether thou be my very son Esau or not.

22 And Jacob went near unto Isaac his father; and he felt him, and said, The voice is Jacob's voice, but the hands are the hands of Esau.

23 And he discerned him not, because his hands were hairy, as his brother Esau's hands: so he blessed him.

24 And he said, Art thou my very son Esau?

And he said, I am.

25 And he said, Bring it near to me, and I will eat of my son's venison, that my soul may bless thee. And he brought it near to him, and he did eat: and he brought him wine and he drank.

26 And his father Isaac said unto him, Come near now, and kiss me, my son.

27 And he came near, and kissed him: and he smelled the smell of his raiment, and blessed him, and said, See, the smell of my son is as the smell of a field which the Lord hath blessed:

28 Therefore God give thee of the dew of heaven, and the fatness of the earth, and plenty of corn and wine:

29 Let people serve thee, and nations bow down to thee: be lord over thy brethren, and let thy mother's sons bow down to thee: cursed be every one that curseth thee, and blessed be he that blesseth thee.

30 And it came to pass, as soon as Isaac had made an end of blessing Jacob, and Jacob was yet scarce gone out from the presence of Isaac his father, that Esau his brother came in from his hunting.

31 And he also had made savoury meat, and brought it unto his father, and said unto his fa-

> ther, Let my father arise, and eat of his son's
> venison, that thy soul may bless me.

Genesis 27, in the opinion of this writer, represents a great wrongdoing on the part of Jacob. When Isaac and Abraham were asked whether or not their wives were really their sisters elsewhere in Genesis, they both told the truth.[53] They did not bear false witness on top of the lies they had told as a matter of conversational technique in the avoidance of being murdered. So, in this way, Genesis 27 gives a clear example of the difference between a fib and a sin. We see the father of lies plying his trade defrauding his father while robbing his brother. Note the contrast between Jacob's excessive self-interest and, for instance, Abraham's interaction with the Lord's priest Melchizedek.[54] Abraham, at that time still Abram, would not accept the priest's gift because he did not want the priest to be able to say, "I made Abram rich."[55] To the contrary, Jacob so far has doubly enriched himself at his own brother's loss with no apparent qualms. By the end of Genesis 27, Jacob has not yet done anything that should explain his alleged favor before the Lord. We see no reason for the Lord to be pleased at all with the one who would be called Israel.

In the account of Isaac's generation, Isaac's wife Rebekah is given approximately equal attention with Isaac, and her scheming nature is spelled out in detail. Satan favors his mother, apparently. After the blessing was stolen, Rebekah heard that Esau planned to kill Jacob.

69

She commanded him to flee to her brother Laban, the son of Abraham's nephew Bethuel. Rebekah told her husband that she would be aggrieved if Jacob took a wife from the Canaanites as Esau had done.[56] By doing so, she was able to manipulate her husband into sending Jacob away for reasons related to finding a wife.[57] In reality, she had already decided to send him away to save him from his brother's vengeance. This story is not so horrible, but, in the context of very few things told about the woman Rebekah, the mother of Satan, she is portrayed as deceitful and manipulative. She and Jacob contrast the cast of characters portrayed in the earlier chapters of Genesis. Earlier, we mostly followed a lineage of righteousness—Noah and Abraham—but with Jacob we have come to another mode of focus.

Genesis 28:20-21 (KJV)

20 And Jacob vowed a vow, saying, If God will be with me, and will keep me in this way that I go, and will give me bread to eat, and raiment to put on, 21 So that I come again to my father's house in peace; then shall the Lord be my God[.]

Jacob made a vow en route to Laban's camp. Again, a stark departure is observed in Jacob's manner from the manner of his forbearers. The vow is conditional. The Lord will be Jacob's god *if* the Lord watches over him.

And *if* the Lord gives him food. And *if* the Lord gives him clothes. Most of the previous prayers in Genesis were reported only as calling on the Lord without the quoted dialogue given, but one imagines that those calls would have been in the form of the prayers which fill the rest of the Bible. Usually prayers take the form, "You are great, Lord. You created all things, and I will do whatever you want." Sometimes such prayers are supplemented with, "but can I please also have this one thing, Lord?"

After Jacob would later receive Laban's two daughters as his wives, he is reported as not loving his wife Leah. This is another derogatory item in the portrayal of Jacob. For God to see that Jacob left his wife Leah so unloved that he made Jacob's preferred wife Rachel barren for many years[58] speaks to some serious character flaw on the part of Jacob. Indeed, in the eventual religion of the Abrahamic nation of the Ishmaelites, Islam, it is required that a man should only marry one wife if he is not going to treat them equally.[59] Here, however, Jacob seems to have relegated Leah as an unwanted stepchild. Later, Jacob would display this same behavior of excessive and inordinate favoritism when he stirred up the ire of his sons against his favorite son Joseph with the gift of a fancy robe.[60] With all of these things: stirring up jealousy among his wives and sons, taking advantage of his brother in a moment of weakness, and stealing his brother's blessing while defrauding his father, one wonders from whence cometh the idea that the Israelites are God's chosen people due to God's great love for Israel. Jacob is no good person. Rather, the Israelites are God's chosen people because his own genetic ancestry comes from among them, and he is forced to protect them as a means of protecting himself. Once God is born into the world, however, the relationship between God and the remaining Israelites will be altered.

While working for his uncle Laban, Jacob's overt lack of righteousness is again displayed with his goat scheme.[61] Laban trusted him to tend the flocks in some fair manner in exchange for the wages he had asked. Then Jacob bred weakness into Laban's flocks. After Laban and his sons noticed that they had been stripped of so much wealth, God told Jacob to return to his native land, allegedly.[62] On the way, God appeared to Jacob in person and fought him at the edge of the river that separated his homeland from the dwelling place of Laban.[63] Since God severely injured Jacob's hip wrestling with him on the far side of the river,[64] we have no reason to think that Jacob was in God's good graces at that time. We will study this encounter more carefully in the next section. Before moving on, it shall suffice to say that Jacob's fording the Jabbok was a sort of crossing the Rubicon moment in the history of the universe. God tried to stop him from crossing but could not or did not. On the other side, Jacob would go on to become Satan. At the river, God changed Jacob's name to Israel.[65]

After crossing the river, Jacob approached the home he had fled. He was afraid that Esau would kill him, so he sent luxurious gifts ahead.[66] In the recounting of the gifts, Jacob sent male and female animals of each kind except for his camels. For the camels, the mightiest of the animals, Jacob only sent females which is consistent with his frame of self-interest. He did not want his brother breeding his own camels.

After Jacob returned home, God spoke to him again. He told him to leave and go to back to Bethel[67] where he had stopped on his earlier flight to Laban in Paddan Aram. In Bethel, the anger of many of Jacob's sons was stirred up against their brother Joseph by their father's gift of a fancy robe.[68] As it was between his wives Leah and Rachel, Jacob was prone to some sort of sick-spirited favoritism. The gift of the robe to Joseph probably was not some trivial act of favoritism in the way that younger children are always spoiled relative to their older siblings.[69] A trivial thing seemingly would not have stirred up the hate of Joseph's brothers to the point where most of them wanted to kill him before they settled on selling him into slavery and lying to their father to say that he had died.[70]

These things were among the actions of the first generation of the Israelites. In Section 15, we will examine the subsequent generations including the two Israelite kingdoms. In brief, the Israelites became slaves in Egypt until the Lord freed them. Even then, they would not stop doing evil. During the reign of King Solomon's son, most of the Israelite tribes rebelled against the house of God's anointed king in Jerusalem. The rebel Kingdom of Israel was evil from its birth and was soon destroyed by the Assyrians. Still, the wickedness of the Israelites remained and grew in the Kingdom of Judah which was eventually destroyed by the Babylonians.

Before Joseph's brothers sold him into slavery, Joseph's account of his dreams stirred up their anger. At first, Joseph dreamt that his brothers' *sheaves* had gathered around his own *sheaf* to bow down to it. Then he dreamt that the stars and the sun and the moon would bow down to him as well.[71] His family was offended, but Joseph's dreams would be doubly borne out. Joseph himself would become ruler in Egypt[72] where he would hold his brothers' fates in his hands,[73] as well as his parents' when they were at risk of starvation in their homeland.[74] Beyond that, King David, whose heir is God himself, was descended from Ephraim:[75] Joseph's son with an Egyptian woman. God's covenant with David[76] would surpass anything between God and the other Israelites. This high status and his mastery in Egypt are well represented in Joseph's dreams.

Notes

[32]Genesis 11:10-26.
[33]Genesis 14:13.
[34]Genesis 11:16.
[35]Genesis 6:3.
[36]Genesis 11:11.
[37] "Twin paradox," https://en.wikipedia.org/wiki/Twin_paradox.
[38]Genesis 12:1-3.
[39]Genesis 13:2.
[40]Genesis 13:14-17.
[41]Genesis 15:5.
[42]Genesis 16:11-12.
[43]Genesis 17:21.

[44]Genesis 18:27-33.

[45]Deuteronomy 23:3.

[46]Ruth 1:4, Ruth 4:17, Matthew 1:6, Luke, 3:31.

[47]Genesis 19. It is recorded that Lot impregnated his daughters unwittingly, but, since Lot himself was a Sodomite reluctant to go where the angels wanted him to go, one wonders if the account of Lot's innocence is accurate. In the Garden, the curse fell on Adam's descendants for Adam's sin, and it would be unusual to find a man in the Bible cursed for his mother's sin.

[48]Genesis 21:8-14.

[49]Genesis 17:19.

[50]Genesis 22:9-12.

[51]Genesis 25:25-26.

[52]Genesis 26:24.

[53]Genesis 12:10-20, Genesis 20:1-13, Genesis 26:7-9.

[54]Genesis 14:18-24.

[55]The account of how Abraham came into his riches is not given in the Bible. One assumes that God blessed Abraham so as to lessen the curse of toil that had fallen on mankind through Adam.

[56]Genesis 27:42-46.

[57]Genesis 28:1-2.

[58]Genesis 29:31.

[59]Koran 4:3.

[60]Genesis 37:3.

[61]Genesis 30:37-43. One notes that Laban had not paid Jacob's wages honestly in a previous labor agreement: Genesis 29:15-25.

[62]Genesis 31:1-3. In Section 16, we will question whether Jacob may have lied about a heavenly command to return home from Laban's camp. It was previously written in Genesis 27:20 that Jacob lied to his father about the Lord giving him a successful hunt, and we will suggest that this was not the only time that Jacob lied about the Lord. To that end, one notes that God's words recorded in Genesis 31:3 differ from the words of the dream Jacob recounts to his wives in Genesis 31:11-13. In the dream, furthermore, it was only an angel of God, not God himself, that told Jacob to depart from Laban.

[63] Genesis 32:24-32.

[64] "Banana Split: Submissions 101," https://www.youtube.co m/watch?v=ZFRZ9B2GubI.

[65] Genesis 32:28.

[66] Genesis 32:13-18.

[67] Genesis 35:1.

[68] Genesis 37:3-4.

[69] These actions may be compared to God's preference for Abel's offering over Cain's in Genesis 4:4. God did not mean to drive Cain into murderous jealousy, but Jacob's excessive favoritism was already recorded between his wives, so the context is somewhat dissimilar.

[70] Genesis 37:28-33.

[71] Genesis 37:5-11.

[72] Genesis 41:41.

[73] Genesis 42:6.

[74] Genesis 43:1-2.

[75] 1 Samuel 17:12.

[76] 2 Samuel 7:8-16.

12. Satan Israel

Now we have reviewed most of what the Bible has to say about the life of Jacob, a.k.a. Israel. About a quarter of Genesis tells his life. Almost everything written portrays him negatively. Jacob preys upon his brother to buy a birthright that Esau may not have wanted to sell. In those events, Esau is reported as despising his birthright, and this note is very strange. In any case, the event of seeming to force the sale of Esau's birthright is one of Jacob's least villainous interactions. At the suggestion of his mother, Jacob defrauds his father to steal rather than buy his brother's blessing. He flees when his mother learns of Esau's intended fratricide. Living with his Uncle Laban, Jacob takes two wives, and God makes his preferred wife Rachel barren for a time when Jacob does not love his first wife Leah. It is not spelled out, but Jacob's lack of love speaks to some severe mistreatment since the man can hardly be faulted for not loving dearly a woman he never wanted to marry.[77]

As with Esau's detested birthright, Laban is not portrayed as any great person while Jacob is with him. Jacob asks for a certain subset of Laban's goats as an honest wage for his continued labors. Then Jacob's character flaw arises. He breeds weakness into the flock that Laban paid him to shepherd. As he had fled from his brother after a previous wrongdoing, Jacob eventually fled from his uncle. Although most of what Israel does in Genesis reeks of a lack of righteousness, the fans and acolytes of Israel will say that the real story is that God loves self-interested, devious schemers, and that too much is read between the lines when we assign Israel as Satan. God does not explicitly tell Israel that his blessing comes to him for Abraham's sake as he had made clear to Isaac. However, the fans of Israel (who must themselves be devious, self-interested schemers[78]) will take the other side in the issue of whether or not more ought to be read into the words of scripture than is plainly written. Such parties will say that God was really blessing Israel for Israel's sake. Therefore, we will begin this section by examining whether or not one ought to read more into the Bible's words than is plainly written.

We may know with absolute certainty that more ought to be read than is plainly written. For example, consider God's covenant of circumcision.[79] Speaking to Abraham, God is quoted as saying little more than that everyone must be circumcised. In reality, God must have given Abraham some specific instructions about what he meant because it would not have sufficed to say, "I want you to cut off part of the penis." The specificity of God's words spoken about circumcision must have far exceeded the quoted dialogue. Another example showing that the reader's insight is required comes from Jacob's time with Laban. Laban uses divination while Jacob is with him,[80] but there is no mention that divination is evil.

Deuteronomy 18:9-12 (NIV)

> **9** When you enter the land the Lord your God is giving you, do not learn to imitate the detestable ways of the nations there. **10** Let no one be found among you who sacrifices their son or daughter in the fire, who practices divination or sorcery, interprets omens, engages in witchcraft, **11** or casts spells, or who is a medium or spiritist or who consults the dead. **12** Anyone who does these things is detestable to the Lord; because of these same detestable practices the Lord your God will drive out those nations before you.

Divination is hated by the Lord. It is forbidden by the Lord's law in Deuteronomy and elsewhere.[81] Even on the last page of the Bible, practitioners of magic arts are cited among the damned.[82] Cover to cover, God hates diviners. Laban's use of divination is a powerful counterexample when Israel's acolytes say that too much interpretation is added in our character study of Jacob as Satan. Their point will be that if Jacob's actions were meant to be understood as indicative of his wickedness, then it would have been written plainly. This line of reasoning is easily refuted with the very brief mention of Laban's use of divination. Throughout the rest of the Bible, God hates divination and magic arts, but Laban's divination is not damned at all. Furthermore, the accounts of the excessive self-interest of Jacob span many chapters in Genesis, and there is little that can be understood as some underlying and/or mitigating righteousness in him.

Jacob's son Joseph uses divination while he is ruler in Egypt.[83] Again, the account is devoid of any context spelling out that God hates it. Indeed, Joseph's silver cup of divination makes a nice segue into how the herder Jacob might have ended up in the advanced technological context of time travel. If magic is to be rejected, meaning that the *magical arts* in the Bible are anachronistic technological feats, then Joseph's silver cup would have been something like a phone with time travel enabled internet, or some such thing. Whatever it was, God hates divination, and that is not recorded in Genesis.

If the herder Jacob became Satan by entering into the fray of time travel, then we must make a technological connection to Jacob's pre-industrial backstory.

Genesis 28:10-19 (NIV)

10 Jacob left Beersheba and set out for Harran. 11 When he reached a certain place, he stopped for the night because the sun had set. Taking one of the stones there, he put it under his head and lay down to sleep. 12 He had a dream in which he saw a stairway resting on the earth, with its top reaching to heaven, and the angels of God were ascending and descending on it. 13 There above it stood the Lord, and he said: "I am the Lord, the God of your father Abraham and the God of Isaac. I will give you and your descen-

dants the land on which you are lying. **14** Your descendants will be like the dust of the earth, and you will spread out to the west and to the east, to the north and to the south. All peoples on earth will be blessed through you and your offspring. **15** I am with you and will watch over you wherever you go, and I will bring you back to this land. I will not leave you until I have done what I have promised you."

16 When Jacob awoke from his sleep, he thought, "Surely the Lord is in this place, and I was not aware of it." **17** He was afraid and said, "How awesome is this place! This is none other than the house of God; this is the gate of heaven."

18 Early the next morning Jacob took the stone he had placed under his head and set it up as a pillar and poured oil on top of it. **19** He called that place Bethel, though the city used to be called Luz.

When Jacob fled from Esau in Beersheba, he had a dream. In the present context, the gate of heaven can lead to nowhere other than the future. In verse 12, Jacob saw the *agents* of God going back and forth through time. Perhaps a temporal portal was present at Bethel: a time machine in a cave perhaps. Maybe it was a nexus of time travel activity of some sort. It is not written that there was a time machine, obviously, and the events are recounted only as a dream. Still, for the time travel interpretation, the agents ascending and descending the stairway to heaven were going to and coming from the future. God's position at the top represents his throne at timelike infinity. Whatever it was that Jacob saw, he was astounded by it, as in verses 16 and 17.

After Jacob returned to his father's home in Beersheba from his uncle's place in Paddan Aram, the means by which he might have become a time traveler may be no more complicated than his use of the time machine the he found on the first leg of his journey. Following Jacob's reunion with Esau, God told him to return there and build an altar.

Genesis 35:1 (KJV)

1 And God said unto Jacob, Arise, go up to Bethel, and dwell there: and make there an altar unto God, that appeared unto thee when thou fleddest from the face of Esau thy brother.

For the purposes of the time travel interpretation, we only suppose that Jacob ended up as a time traveler somehow. To support that, we will briefly speculate far and wide about how those events may have unfolded.

What was the altar Jacob built at the gate of heaven? Perhaps it was a time machine built at a temporal nexus. Perhaps it was an altar in the usual sense constructed at the place where a time machine was already installed. Perhaps it was Esau's birthright as the elder son to serve the Lord as a time agent, and this is what Jacob purchased from him. When Jacob bought his brother's birthright, Esau was described as a skillful hunter and a man of the *open country*.[84] It is reasonable to assume that this was a skill in the ordinary sense of hunting, but one must also assume that the general work of time agents would have been *hunting* the rebels who were using time travel for purposes other than the furtherance of God's plan. If Esau did not care for such work, then he may have detested it and been glad to be rid of such duties. Whatever the case may be, building the connection between Jacob the herder and Satan the time traveler is the biggest leap required for the study undertaken here. We do not know how it happened. We have contextualized the likelihood for technological possibilities, both in the presence of devices of divination and the presence of a gate to *the future*, but the moment where Jacob first set foot at a time other than his own is not easily identified. In the remainder of this section, we will continue to motivate the idea that Jacob did take that step at some point in his 147 years, and that his excessive self-interest motivated a Satanic rebellion in which he tried to replace the Lord at the top of the stairway he had seen.

The question regarding why the Holy Spirit would allow Jacob to enter the time machine is a difficult one. The Bible tells us that the mind of God is unknowable, but we may speculate as we have throughout this analysis. Fundamentally, though it is dark and may appear cruel, this writer can find no better explanation than the words of the painter Bob Ross: it is not possible to paint a highlight without painting a shadow. If God found that a rebellion was inevitable, meaning that someone would always be tempted to test their luck if not warned by the rotting corpses of those who had already tried and failed,[85] then placing the rebellion at the earliest possible time would cause the fewest number of people to fall under its spell. As the master of all creation, these are the kinds of big picture issues that set the mind of God in Heaven, who is called the Holy Spirit, apart from the thinking of mere mortals. Eventually, the devil was cast down to *the earth* because he was not strong enough to unseat the Lord.[86] At that time, he may have walked out onto the land in Bethel where the rest of his life would unfold as documented in the remainder of Genesis. Perhaps the password he bought from his brother would no longer activate the device he had found.

The Bible's most abnormal story about God, excepting possibly Isaac's sacrifice, comes on the far bank of the Jabbok as Jacob goes toward his reunion with Esau.

Genesis 32:22-32 (NIV)

22 That night Jacob got up and took his two wives, his two female servants and his eleven sons and crossed the ford of the Jabbok. 23 After he had sent them across the stream, he sent over all

his possessions. 24 So Jacob was left alone, and a man wrestled with him till daybreak. 25 When the man saw that he could not overpower him, he touched the socket of Jacob's hip so that his hip was wrenched as he wrestled with the man. 26 Then the man said, "Let me go, for it is daybreak."

But Jacob replied, "I will not let you go unless you bless me."

27 The man asked him, "What is your name?"

"Jacob," he answered.

28 Then the man said, "Your name will no longer be Jacob, but Israel, because you have struggled with God and with humans and have overcome."

29 Jacob said, "Please tell me your name."

But he replied, "Why do you ask my name?" Then he blessed him there.

30 So Jacob called the place Peniel, saying, "It is because I saw God face to face, and yet my life was spared."

31 The sun rose above him as he passed Peniel, and he was limping because of his hip. 32 Therefore to this day the Israelites do not eat the tendon attached to the socket of the hip, because the socket of Jacob's hip was touched near the tendon.

Sometimes the encounter in Genesis 32 is described as an altercation between Jacob and an angel. Sometimes it is taken to record an encounter with God himself. Here, we take the view that Jacob wrestled with the man God. Although it is written that God told Jacob to return home,[87] it appears that God did not want Jacob to cross the river. These events may be reconciled in two ways: God told Jacob to return before he learned of Jacob's rebellion, or God never told him to return at all.[88] After Satan's evil was revealed, God wanted to kill him on the far side of the river to prevent the rebellion. Perhaps God went straight from the river to Abraham with his order to kill Isaac. Perhaps events unfolded oppositely so that God went on from the near sacrifice of Isaac to test whether his kingdom would hold if he let the Israelites cross the river before slaying Jacob on the other side. Whatever the context was, the injury to Jacob's hip is good evidence that Jacob was not in God's good graces at the encounter by the Jabbok.

The limping injury in verse 31 is somewhat evocative of God's curse on the serpent in the Garden.[89] In any case, God could not or did not kill Jacob. By the end of all things, the wisdom of the Spirit of God was that it was better to let Jacob cross than to stop him at the river. Seeing that Jacob would live, God changed his name to Israel. The NIV footnote to verse 28 is, "*Israel* probably means *he struggles with God.*" Here we take *Israel* to mean *he fights against God.* It is taken for granted that the one who fights against God is Satan.

Before Israel crossed the river, he asked for his opponent's name. Although God is elsewhere forthcoming with his name and his identity as the God of Jacob's ancestors, God says on the side of the river with disdain, "Man! Why are you asking my name?!" It does not say in the scripture that God said this with disdain, but the disdain is plain to this writer. We take the context to be that God knew Jacob would go on to become Satan, and it was too bitter for him to say, "I am your protector, Jacob. I am God, the one you will betray." God hurt Jacob's hip severely enough that the Israelites enacted a prohibition against eating a certain cut of meat. The enduring prohibition cited in verse 32 suggests that Jacob bore this injury for the rest of his days. Again, this is at least somewhat evocative of God's curse that the serpent should crawl. Perhaps the words for crawling and limping were the same in the original tongue.

When morning came, God had to tell Israel to let him go, and this is a most abnormal account of God. Jacob said he would let him go only if he would receive a blessing. While this story again emphasizes that the man God is not omnipotent, and that the quality of omnipotence should be confined to the Spirit of God, it may be the only time that God is portrayed as something other than very mighty.[90]

Another interpretation for the wrestling between God and Jacob is that future Jacob—Satan—and God fought over whether or not history would allow Jacob to cross the river. In this sense, the abatement of the wrestling at daybreak is given in the context of day and night in the story of creation, or the day shift and the night shift.

They wrestled over what history would be until it was determined that it was better to let Jacob cross. The establishment of this fact would be called the break of day: the determination of what was good. Supporting this alternative to literal wrestling, even Olympic athletes would be hard-pressed to wrestle all night, potentially eight hours or more. In the frame of the story of creation, the day is good, and the night is evil. It follows that wrestling until daybreak would symbolize the jostling of timelines as Satan and God overwrote each other until it was determined by the Spirit of God that it was better to allow Israel to cross the Jabbok. In this way, the eccentricity of God's inability to defeat Jacob in a wrestling match vanishes. In the end, God himself allows Jacob to cross when he finds that the future which comes from stopping him is not preferable. Eventually, God told Jacob to let him go, and Jacob refused unless he would receive a blessing. It is hard to know what this means. Satan was very strong, apparently.

Genesis 35:9-10 (KJV)

9 And God appeared unto Jacob again, when he came out of Padanaram, and blessed him. 10 And God said unto him, Thy name is Jacob: thy name shall not be called any more Jacob, but Israel shall be thy name: and he called his name Israel.

In Genesis 35, a while after Israel crossed the river and was reunited with his brother, God again reminded Jacob that his name had been changed to Israel. In verse ten, the NIV attaches a footnote to the name Jacob reading, "*Jacob* means *he grasps the heel*, a Hebrew idiom for *he deceives.*" Some in the world will take such things to mean that God loves deception, and that he hurt Jacob's hip because he loved Jacob so much for the way he did wrong to his brother and father and uncle and wife. In the present interpretation, we understand that Jacob's name became an idiomatic expression meaning *he deceives* because Israel is the father of lies who is also called Satan, the devil, the morning star, the serpent, and the dragon. The fact that God named him Israel a second time is consistent with the interpretation of wrestling as overwriting histories. Perhaps God named him Israel for the first time in Genesis 35, and it was only when Satan demanded a blessing at the end of the wrestling in Genesis 32 that God again raised the matter of Satan's name: Fights Against God.[91]

Regarding Satan's name, consider God's pronouncement against the serpent in the Garden.[92] God said, "You will strike his heel." Later, when Satan was born, he was named *He Grasps the Heel*.[93] More likely than a reference to an injured foot, God foretold Satan's name in the Garden with words that meant, "You will be *He Grasps the Heel.*" As between *fights* and *struggles* in the Hebrew meaning of the name Israel, we make a similar appeal to conflation among *grasps* and *strikes*. One imagines a simpler word meaning to extend or use the hand.

89

Genesis 46:1-4 (NIV)

1 So Israel set out with all that was his, and when he reached Beersheba, he offered sacrifices to the God of his father Isaac.

2 And God spoke to Israel in a vision at night and said, "Jacob! Jacob!"

"Here I am," he replied.

3 "I am God, the God of your father," he said. "Do not be afraid to go down to Egypt, for I will make you into a great nation there. 4 I will go down to Egypt with you, and I will surely bring you back again. And Joseph's own hand will close your eyes."

Although God had told Israel about his new name twice before the events of Genesis 46, here God calls him Jacob and speaks to him kindly. We suggest that God in Genesis 46 is speaking to Israel from a time in his own life prior to his discovery of Satan's rebellion, and before he would later change Jacob's name to Israel. It is understood that one might use a time machine to go back to April from September but then, later, go back to January from October. We suggest this is the reason why God used the name Jacob at the late time in Genesis 46.

One possible chronology of events would be as follows. After Jacob's mother sent him away to avoid being murdered by his brother, God appeared to him and told him that he would be with him, that he would deliver the Promised Land to his descendants, and that those descendants would become uncountably many.[94] Jacob then said that God will be his god *if* the Lord meets certain conditions.[95] Later, Jacob was again forced to flee having defrauded Laban in more or less the same manner he had defrauded his brother and father. At a later time recounted in Genesis 46, God saw that Jacob was in his own land again and said that it would be alright for him to go down to Egypt. He reiterated his promises using the name Jacob. After that, God used his time machine to check on how Jacob had gotten back to his own land after God had taken him out of it. During that time, God saw Jacob's goat fraud and ordered him to return home for his own safety...or not; Jacob had already lied about God when he told his father that the Lord had given him success in a hunt he never went on,[96] so he may have lied to his wives about receiving instructions to depart from Paddan Aram as well. On the timeline which followed their departure, God saw that Jacob would become Satan. He tried to stop Jacob from crossing the river and was not able to do so, or eventually chose not to do so, because the alternatives were worse. In the end, the weeds were left in the field. One speculates that there was always an eventual rebellion on the timelines where Satan's rebellion was quashed. Allowing Satan to cross the river was preferable to stopping him.

In Section 9 regarding the time travel war, the conclusion of the matter was not that the devil was killed.

The devil was hurled down to the earth[97] meaning that Israel was sent back to his own place in history. When it says that the serpent lost his place in heaven, we are told that Jacob lost whatever time travel capability he would gain on the other side of the Jabbok. When Jacob was old and about to die, he told his sons what their futures would be.[98] How might Israel have known what would happen in the future if he was not using a time machine? Israel was hardly a prophet, and it does not say that the Word of God came to him about his sons' futures. Indeed, the rest of the future of the Israelites recorded in the Bible shows that Israel got it very wrong regarding his prophecy on what would become of the many tribes bearing his name. The false telling of his sons' fortunes may be the strongest evidence of the lack of good faith between Israel and God. The future Israel foretold was not the one that came to pass. Israel got it wrong. After he died, God was still working to change things for the better.

Deuteronomy 18:21-22 (KJV)

21 And if thou say in thine heart, How shall we know the word which the Lord hath not spoken? 22 When a prophet speaketh in the name of the Lord, if the thing follow not, nor come to pass, that is the thing which the Lord hath not spoken, but the prophet hath spoken it presumptuously:

> thou shalt not be afraid of him.

For all of his sons except Simeon and Levi, Satan gave their fortunes individually.[99] For Simeon and Levi, he put the two brothers together and prophesied that they would be scattered for their violence. Their fates would be the same. Satan said he did not want to be in council with them. However, the fates of the Simeonites and the Levites would turn out to be quite different. The words of the false prophet failed.

Exodus 32:25-29 (NIV)

25 Moses saw that the people were running wild and that Aaron had let them get out of control and so become a laughingstock to their enemies. 26 So he stood at the entrance to the camp and said, "Whoever is for the Lord, come to me." And all the Levites rallied to him.

27 Then he said to them, "This is what the Lord, the God of Israel, says: 'Each man strap a sword to his side. Go back and forth through the camp from one end to the other, each killing his brother and friend and neighbor.'" 28 The Levites did as Moses commanded, and that day about three thousand of the people died. 29 Then Moses said, "You have been set apart to

> the Lord today, for you were against your own sons and brothers, and he has blessed you this day."

After Satan died, his descendants became slaves in Egypt as God had promised Abraham.[100] Perhaps the enslavement of the Israelites was punishment for Israel's rebellion. Centuries passed, and then the Lord sent Moses to free them from Pharaoh's yoke. Then they wandered in the wilderness for 40 years. During that time, Moses went up on the mountain to receive the ten commandments from God.[101] When he came back, the Israelites had abandoned the Lord to worship a golden calf,[102] as in verse 25. When Moses called for whomever was for the Lord, the Levites answered him. They took up arms and killed their brothers and sons and friends and neighbors because they were worshiping the idol. Then they were blessed for the violence that Satan had prophesied would be their undoing.[103]

Deuteronomy 18:1-2 (KJV)

1 The priests the Levites, and all the tribe of Levi, shall have no part nor inheritance with Israel: they shall eat the offerings of the Lord made by fire, and his inheritance. 2 Therefore shall they have no inheritance among their brethren:

> the Lord is their inheritance, as he hath said unto them.

At the end of the Israelites' time in the wilderness—at the time of the inheritance of the land—the Levites received no land. Every tribe other than the Levites came into possession of land taken from the Canaanites, but the Levites' inheritance was to be the Lord's priests. Therefore, we should consider Satan's words for them.

Genesis 49:5-7 (NIV)

5   "Simeon and Levi are brothers—
        their swords are weapons of violence.
6   Let me not enter their council,
        let me not join their assembly,
    for they have killed men in their anger
        and hamstrung oxen as they pleased.
7   Cursed be their anger, so fierce,
        and their fury, so cruel!
    I will scatter them in Jacob
        and disperse them in Israel.

Satan did not mention God's everlasting covenant with the Levites that they should minister before the

Lord forever as his priests. The third book of the Bible—
The Third Book of Moses, called Leviticus—is named
after the Levites due to the blessing they received on
account of their violence in service to the Lord. Satan
thought this violence would be a problem for them, and
that their fate was so unremarkable that it should be
lumped in with the fate of the Simeonites. The future
that Satan had seen was not the one that came to pass.
The Lord undermined him. The conclusion of Satan's
story was that he told his sons the wrong thing. He
proved his foolishness at the end of a life of wickedness.
Then he died after many years eating the Lord's dust.

In the present day, there exists a country named after
Satan. Israeli scholars must know very well that they are
Satanists (or else they are deluded to the point of willful
ignorance.) The Jews have the Christians and Paulites
(and others) mostly convinced that God loves Satan, and
that God and *Fights Against God* are best friends. At his
birth, Jacob's name meant *he grasps the heel*. It would
become an idiom meaning *he deceives*, and now many
of the children of Satan continue in the tradition of deception of their father via the political power afforded to
them through the governing bodies of the secular state
of *Satan*.

Isaiah 44:24-25 (NIV)

24 "This is what the Lord says—

> your Redeemer, who formed you in the
> womb:
>
> I am the Lord,
>   the Maker of all things,
>   who stretches out the heavens,
>   who spreads out the earth by myself,
> 25   who foils the signs of false prophets
>   and makes fools of diviners,
>   who overthrows the learning of the wise
>   and turns it into nonsense[.]

Isaiah 44 tells what God did to Israel. He foiled his false prophecy.

Notes

[77]Genesis 29:22.

[78]The noncanonical and wrong proverb, "God helps those who help themselves," probably comes from the school of Israel.

[79]Genesis 17:1-14.

[80]Genesis 30:27.

[81]E.g.: 2 Kings 17:17, 1 Samuel 15:23, Zechariah 10:2, Micah 3:7-11, Malachi 3:5, etc.

[82]Revelation 22:15.

[83]Genesis 44:5.

[84]Genesis 25:27-34.

[85]Isaiah 66:24.

[86]Revelation 12:7-8.

[87]Genesis 31:3.

[88]In Section 16, we will offer a simpler version of events leading to Jacob's encounter with God near the river. We will present the

case that Jacob may have lied about receiving new instructions from the Lord.

[89] Genesis 3:14-15.

[90] *Very mighty* is another meaning of the word *almighty* besides *omnipotent*.

[91] Whether one takes *Israel* to mean *he struggles with God* or *he fights with God*, Isaiah 45:9 gives the warning, "Woe unto him that striveth with his maker." Both meanings for Israel's name mean *he strives with God*.

[92] Genesis 3:15.

[93] Genesis 25:26.

[94] Genesis 28:13-14.

[95] Genesis 28:20-21.

[96] Genesis 27:20.

[97] Revelation 12:9.

[98] Genesis 49:1-28.

[99] Genesis 49:5-7:

[100] Genesis 15:13.

[101] Exodus 19:20.

[102] In the present day, the image of the calf worshiped by the Israelites is a uniquely sanctified article of the Hindu religion which does not revere the Lord.

[103] Exodus 32:25-29.

13. Satan in the Bible

There are few direct mentions of *Satan* in the Bible. One would think that the character whose name is Fights Against God would be featured as prominently in the book as he is in the minds of those who read and teach from it, but that is not the case...unless Israel is Satan. In that case, most of the Bible is a chronicle of the interactions between God and the children of Satan: the Israelites. Since Israel's true identity is little appreciated, the noncanonical knowledge that the greatest trick the devil ever pulled was to convince the world of his nonexistence is consistent with the modern take on the Bible.

Revelation 22:18-21 (KJV)

18 For I testify unto every man that heareth the words of the prophecy of this book, If any man shall add unto these things, God shall add unto him the plagues that are written in this book: 19 And if any man shall take away from the words of the book of this prophecy, God shall take away his part out of the book of life, and out of the holy city, and from the things which are written in this book.

20 He which testifieth these things saith, Surely I come quickly. Amen. Even so, come, Lord Jesus.

> **21** The grace of our Lord Jesus Christ be with you all. Amen.

The last four verses of the last book of The Holy Bible, the final words of the 66th of 66 books, give a warning against changing the text. We suppose that the Bible would not conclude with these words if alterations had not already been a problem in history. For instance, Satan may have edited the worst parts of his story out of the history of the Israelites who were not only his descendants but were also the scribes that first recorded the words and edited them later. As an example of a place where the original scroll may have been altered, we suggest Isaiah 14.

Isaiah 14:1-27 (NIV)

1 The Lord will have compassion on Jacob;
        once again he will choose Israel
        and will settle them in their own land.
    Foreigners will join them
        and unite with the descendants of Jacob.
2 Nations will take them
        and bring them to their own place.
    And Israel will take possession of the nations
        and make them male and female servants

in the Lord's land.
They will make captives of their captors
and rule over their oppressors.

3 On the day the Lord gives you relief from your
suffering and turmoil and from the harsh labor
forced on you, 4 you will take up this taunt
against the king of Babylon:

How the oppressor has come to an end!
How his fury has ended!
5   The Lord has broken the rod of the wicked,
the scepter of the rulers,
6   which in anger struck down peoples
with unceasing blows,
and in fury subdued nations
with relentless aggression.
7   All the lands are at rest and at peace;
they break into singing.
8   Even the junipers and the cedars of Lebanon
gloat over you and say,
"Now that you have been laid low,
no one comes to cut us down."

9   The realm of the dead below is all astir
to meet you at your coming;
it rouses the spirits of the departed to greet
you—
all those who were leaders in the world;
it makes them rise from their thrones—
all those who were kings over the nations.

10   They will all respond,
         they will say to you,
      "You also have become weak, as we are;
         you have become like us."
11   All your pomp has been brought down to
      the grave,
         along with the noise of your harps;
      maggots are spread out beneath you
         and worms cover you.

12   How you have fallen from heaven,
         morning star, son of the dawn!
      You have been cast down to the earth,
         you who once laid low the nations!
13   You said in your heart,
         "I will ascend to the heavens;
      I will raise my throne
         above the stars of God;
      I will sit enthroned on the mount of assem-
      bly,
         on the utmost heights of Mount Zaphon.
14   I will ascend above the tops of the clouds;
         I will make myself like the Most High."
15   But you are brought down to the realm of
      the dead,
         to the depths of the pit.

16   Those who see you stare at you,
         they ponder your fate:
      "Is this the man who shook the earth

and made kingdoms tremble,
17 the man who made the world a wilderness,
who overthrew its cities
and would not let his captives go home?"

18 All the kings of the nations lie in state,
each in his own tomb.
19 But you are cast out of your tomb
like a rejected branch;
you are covered with the slain,
with those pierced by the sword,
those who descend to the stones of the pit.
Like a corpse trampled underfoot,
20 you will not join them in burial,
for you have destroyed your land
and killed your people.

Let the offspring of the wicked
never be mentioned again.
21 Prepare a place to slaughter his children
for the sins of their ancestors;
they are not to rise to inherit the land
and cover the earth with their cities.

22 "I will rise up against them,"
declares the Lord Almighty.
"I will wipe out Babylon's name and survivors,
her offspring and descendants,"
declares the Lord.
23 "I will turn her into a place for owls

and into swampland;
I will sweep her with the broom of destruction,"
declares the Lord Almighty.

24 The Lord Almighty has sworn,

"Surely, as I have planned, so it will be,
and as I have purposed, so it will happen.
25 I will crush the Assyrian in my land;
on my mountains I will trample him down.
His yoke will be taken from my people,
and his burden removed from their shoulders."

26 This is the plan determined for the whole world;
this is the hand stretched out over all nations.
27 For the Lord Almighty has purposed, and who can thwart him?
His hand is stretched out, and who can turn it back?

We have included more text than bears on the issue of adding or taking away words because the entire passage is germane to the time travel interpretation. The context at the beginning of Isaiah 14 is that Isaiah continues a prophecy begun in the previous chapter.[104] Following the usual formatting, it is not clear whether the continued prophecy ends at verse two or if extends through verse 27.

Namely, it is not clear if the taunt is part of the previous prophecy or if something else is written at the paragraph break starting with verse three. In the opinion of this writer, this "taunt" is not a prophecy. Within the taunt, we suppose that the ambiguity in the attribution of the pronouns—the various instances of *you*—suggests that the version of Isaiah 14 known in the modern day is not the version recorded in earliest antiquity. Indeed, many scholars' previous analyses have found that the modern Book of Isaiah underwent extensive editing[105] following its initial binding by the scribes of King Hezekiah: the last of the kings of Judah to receive prophecy from Isaiah.

Regarding the taunt begun in verse four, consider the following. At first, the king of Babylon is referenced with the third person possessive pronoun *his*. In verse eight, the king of Babylon is called *you*, but it fits the context of a taunt that he might have been addressed at first in the third person. With the paragraph break going into verses nine through 11, we continue with the second person *you*. While these verses seem well levied against a fallen king, the mention of the realm of the dead below makes a certain appeal to the realm of the past. Numerous kings had already fallen before the Lord, so there is not yet any strong reason to suspect that *you* refers to someone other than the king of Babylon. By verse 12, however, *you* most certainly references the devil. The language about being cast down to the earth was the same in Section 9 when we studied Satan's fall from heaven.[106] In verses 13 and 14, the language attributed to *you* is the same from Jacob's dream at Bethel.[107] It is our present thesis that sometime after Satan departed from Laban, he entered the fray of time travel intending to replace the Lord at the top of the stairway to heaven where the angels were ascending and descending. Our character study of Satan shows that if he were made aware of a gateway to heaven, he would have passed through it for the nourishment of his excessive self-interest. After he did so and failed to unseat the Lord, he lost his access to the stairway and was cast down into "the realm of the dead below," which is the past. This context suggests that an indictment against the devil was spliced into the taunt against the king of Babylon starting at verse nine.

Verse 12 contains the first Biblical mention of the morning star, or the son of the dawn. From the context in which the morning star seeks to replace God, we understand that this is Satan: the one who fights against God. To the extent of the confusion of the pronouns, perhaps Satan set himself as the king of Babylon in his rebellion. Possibly the original scrolls were sliced and diced beyond the proto-, deutero-, and trito-Isaiah splices that are generally accepted in modern academic circles of Biblical scholarship.[108] The pronouns would be confused because some clear language about the identity of Satan appeared in the original text but was lost over time. As it is said but not written in any scripture that survived until the modern era: the greatest trick the devil ever pulled was to convince the world that he doesn't exist.

In verses 12 through 15, *you* was fallen from the future. He is called the morning star possibly because his works are the works that remain when the console's day shift comes to work in the morning. Perhaps the epithet references daybreak by the Jabbok when the Spirit of God determined that the final course of history should not prevent Satan's rebellion.[109] In verse 13, *you* seeks to ascend to the utmost heights which must be understood as the seat of ultimate victory at timelike infinity. In verse 14, *you* seeks to make himself like the most high. God has the name *the most high* in the present interpretation for many reasons including that timelike infinity is the most future-directed point in the universe. There is no time later than timelike infinity. In verse 15, *you* fails to have supplanted God, but nowhere in the prophets or the histories of the kings of Israel and Judah are we told of any king of Babylon trying to become God. Hence, we will presume that a different person than the king of Babylon is the morning star cited in verse 12.

In verses 16 and 17, it appears that *you* is no longer the devil but is rather God himself, in the opinion of this writer. Earlier in Isaiah, God is referred to as the one who shakes the Earth.[110] Many times in the Bible, God is referred to as the one who hates and destroys cities and makes the world a wilderness.[111] It is not fitting to think that *you* at this point could be either of the king of Babylon or the morning star. By verse 24, the Lord is wiping out the Assyrians, and it is clear that we can no longer be in the taunt against the king of Babylon. However, there is no other context given. For all of these reasons, we cite Isaiah 14 as an example of what Jesus Christ warned about in Revelation 22: adding words or removing them from the text. We suggest that a direct attribution of Israel as Satan does not appear in the Bible because the words have been changed over time. Beyond that, John of Patmos saw certain things that he was told not to write in Revelation because they would not be revealed until the end. The identity of Satan as Abraham's grandson may be one of those things.

If the Word of God is perfect, then how can it be sabotaged?

Isaiah 55:8-13 (NIV)

8 "For my thoughts are not your thoughts,
    neither are your ways my ways,"
        declares the Lord.
9 "As the heavens are higher than the earth,
    so are my ways higher than your ways
    and my thoughts than your thoughts.
10 As the rain and the snow
    come down from heaven,
and do not return to it
    without watering the earth
and making it bud and flourish,
    so that it yields seed for the sower and
    bread for the eater,
11 so is my word that goes out from my mouth:
    It will not return to me empty,
but will accomplish what I desire
    and achieve the purpose for which I sent

> it.
> 12 You will go out in joy
>   and be led forth in peace;
>   the mountains and hills
>   will burst into song before you,
>   and all the trees of the field
>   will clap their hands.
> 13 Instead of the thornbush will grow the juniper,
>   and instead of briers the myrtle will grow.
>   This will be for the Lord's renown,
>   for an everlasting sign,
>   that will endure forever."

In Isaiah 55, God promises that his word will achieve all for which he has purposed it. We are called to understand that the Bible is sufficient to ensure that God reaps the good seed at the time of the harvest, and that he will burn the weeds in the fire.[112]

Aside from the issue of Satanic agents splicing scrolls, there are other things in the Bible that show the text cannot be taken literally at all times. At the end of 1 Samuel, for instance, Saul takes his own life.[113] At the beginning of 2 Samuel, an Amalekite reports that he killed Saul himself.[114] Both accounts can't be true. One thing being reported as an event and the other as a claim might lead us to resolve the contradiction by the Amalekite's lie, but there are other hints as well. The accounts of the fate of Judas Iscariot constitute one such further example.[115]

109

By now, we have motivated a scenario which may explain the small number of Satan's direct mentions in the Bible. If he isn't the most mentioned character, Satan, who is called Israel, is the second most mentioned character. In the remainder of this section, we will examine a few of the direct mentions while saving an important one for Section 20.

Job 1:6-12 (NIV)

6 One day the angels came to present themselves before the Lord, and Satan also came with them. 7 The Lord said to Satan, "Where have you come from?"

Satan answered the Lord, "From roaming throughout the earth, going back and forth on it."

8 Then the Lord said to Satan, "Have you considered my servant Job? There is no one on earth like him; he is blameless and upright, a man who fears God and shuns evil."

9 "Does Job fear God for nothing?" Satan replied. 10 "Have you not put a hedge around him and his household and everything he has? You have blessed the work of his hands, so that his flocks and herds are spread throughout the land. 11 But now stretch out your hand and

> strike everything he has, and he will surely curse you to your face."
>
> **12** The Lord said to Satan, "Very well, then, everything he has is in your power, but on the man himself do not lay a finger."
>
> Then Satan went out from the presence of the Lord.

In Job 1, Satan is in the company of God's agents. We suggest that this interaction between God and Satan took place after Satan had rebelled against God, but before God learned of what he had done. Satan's comments about going back and forth on the Earth should refer to his time traveling attempts to undermine God by sowing his weeds throughout history. Equivalently, Satan's roaming should be his ascending and descending on the stairs he had seen at Bethel. The devil is called the accuser in Revelation,[116] and here we find Satan accusing Job of impiety. Satan's accusations were wrongful. The main point of The Book of Job is that Job never acted as Satan said he would. Job was a righteous man, and Satan was a liar.[117]

The story of Job is one of the worst stories in the Bible, in the opinion of this writer. The cruelty and suffering is presented as a nearly senseless tragedy. At the end, Job's fortune is restored. He is gifted with new children, but an apparently needless and great suffering was foisted upon him. Job spent a long time in misery.

Job 38:1-18 (NIV)

1 Then the Lord spoke to Job out of the storm.
He said:

2   "Who is this that obscures my plans
        with words without knowledge?

3   Brace yourself like a man;
        I will question you,
        and you shall answer me.

4   "Where were you when I laid the earth's
    foundation?
        Tell me, if you understand.

5   Who marked off its dimensions? Surely you
    know!
        Who stretched a measuring line across it?

6   On what were its footings set,
        or who laid its cornerstone—

7   while the morning stars sang together
        and all the angels shouted for joy?

8   "Who shut up the sea behind doors
        when it burst forth from the womb,

9   when I made the clouds its garment
        and wrapped it in thick darkness,

10   when I fixed limits for it
        and set its doors and bars in place,

11   when I said, 'This far you may come and no
    farther;

here is where your proud waves halt'?

12 "Have you ever given orders to the morning,
    or shown the dawn its place,
13 that it might take the earth by the edges
    and shake the wicked out of it?
14 The earth takes shape like clay under a seal;
    its features stand out like those of a gar-
    ment.
15 The wicked are denied their light,
    and their upraised arm is broken.

16 "Have you journeyed to the springs of the
    sea
    or walked in the recesses of the deep?
17 Have the gates of death been shown to you?
    Have you seen the gates of the deepest
    darkness?
18 Have you comprehended the vast expanses
    of the earth?
    Tell me, if you know all this.

Job 38 is remarkable in its amenability to the time travel interpretation. Verses four through six speak to some specific technical mastery on the part of the Lord. If we take God as the man who invented the first time machine, whose near invincibility in the time travel war would have been guaranteed by such a feat, then these verses might refer to his work in physics. When the war was over, the Spirit of God remained at the end of time.

Then God went to the beginning to mark off the dimensions of history with a bloodline stretching from Adam through Noah, Abraham, Satan, David, Solomon, and onward through the line of David. Eventually, history must come to God himself and those who will come later to use the time machine like Michael the archangel did when he fought for God's intentions and against God's adversaries.[118] Verses seven and 12 both have direct bearing on the battle for control between the day shift and the night shift. In the morning, someone issues the marching orders, and here God implies that he has given such orders. In verses 16 and 17, God asks if Job has gone far into the past, possibly as far as the time of turmoil before creation to see how horrible things might have been.

As remarkable as the story of Job is, God's chastisement in Job 38 is remarkable as well. In the preceding chapters, Job opines on the injustice of his situation, and his friends share their opinions. After the wrong explanations of Job's friends and Job's own lamentation of his inability to understand, God interjects himself into the conversation citing his technical mastery in the most certain terms to appear anywhere in the Bible. The correct interpretation for Job's plight is given by the Parable of the Weeds: God did not undo the actions that followed from Israel's direct lie to God's face. Furthermore, this story featuring Satan so prominently and it being the first Biblical instance of dialogue attributed to Satan by name, it may have been instrumental in the instruction of the Living God by the Spirit of God. By Job's righteousness, Satan was revealed to God as a liar, and God

114

would later make a fool of Satan on his deathbed when he told his children the wrong future.

To support the instrumental instruction interpretation for The Book of Job, one must note its eccentricity with respect to the Bible's other accounts of the Lord. Job is a terrible tragedy of extended human suffering unlike any other book in the Bible. It begins with the first dialogue attributed to the person of Satan. The apparent initial condition is that Satan is in God's good graces. These things contrast the usual telling of things in the Bible and support an interpretation in which Job's suffering formed a uniquely important account in the story of the Lord. We suggest Job's suffering was not pointless, but that it was instrumental in the increase of the knowledge of the Living God. Somehow, God had to learn what Satan was doing. Perhaps the revelation of Satan's lie served that purpose when Job never cursed God. If so, this gives context to the harshness of the words spoken by God in Job 38. God chastised Job for not understanding his plan which may have relied upon Job's righteousness in some large part. Satan told God that Job would curse the Lord to his face, but Job never did. Satan lied to God from within God's own assembly, and God saw the lie. This is the most detailed interaction between God and Satan anywhere in the Bible: God caught Satan lying.

To close this section, we give the strongest evidence that Israel is Satan: direct words to that effect in the Bible. While Satan has been able in history to corrupt the knowledge of many believers who find a general soli-

115

darity between God and Fights Against God, Satan was not able to corrupt the record to the point where his identity was no longer written.

---

1 Chronicles 21:1 (NIV)

1 Satan rose up against Israel and incited David to take a census of Israel.

---

2 Samuel 24:1 (NIV)

1 Again the anger of the Lord burned against Israel, and he incited David against them, saying, "Go and take a census of Israel and Judah."

Satan is only mentioned in the Bible once before The Book of Job. In 1 Chronicles 21, Satan was able to incite David to take a census of Israel. The account of the same census written in 2 Samuel 24 is usually taken as a conflicting account in which it was God who told David to take the census. Recalling that Israel is the man Satan himself and not only a nation under King David, the two accounts are reconciled when *he* is Israel. If 2 Samuel 24's *he* refers to the Lord, then one account is wrong, and this exceeds the contradiction between the words of the Amalekite in 2 Samuel and Saul's suicide in 1 Samuel. The death of King Saul may have had different accounts recorded honestly in the way that historians sometimes do not know the true account of things on the battlefield. Possibly we are to understand that the Amalekite lied, and that the contradiction is resolved in that way. However, there is no possible (reasonable) reconciliation between the divergent accounts of David's census if *he* is the Lord in 2 Samuel 24. If *he* is Satan, whose name is Israel, however, then there is no contradiction. These two verses should be understood to state that Israel is Satan without any reference to the many suggestions written here!

Notes

[104]Isaiah 13:1.

[105]"Book of Isaiah," https://en.wikipedia.org/wiki/Book_o f_Isaiah.

[106]Revelation 12:9-10.

[107]Genesis 28:12.

[108]E.g.: Duhm, Bernhard. *The Book of Isaiah Translated and Explained (Das Buch Jesaia übersetzt und erklärt)*, 1892.

[109]Genesis 32:26.

[110]Isaiah 2:19-21, Isaiah 5:25, Isaiah 13:9-13.

[111]E.g.: Genesis 19:29, Leviticus 26:31, 2 Kings 19:25, Isaiah 5:5-6, Jeremiah 48:8, Ezekiel 35:4, Micah 5:14, etc.

[112]In the collection of the weeds, The Parable of the Weeds lends itself to the noncanonical notion of a grim reaper.

[113]1 Samuel 31:4.

[114]2 Samuel 1:10.

[115]Matthew 27:1-5, Acts 1:18.

[116]Revelation 12:10.

[117]Where one might be tempted to read an English-specific Bible code in the name Satan Israel as *Satan is real*, one might also take

note of the name of the Jabbok river as commemorating that *Job is ok*. Indeed, even the names *Jacob* and *Jabbok* seem too close for pure coincidence.

[118]Revelation 12:7.

14. The Satanic Thesis

Now we have made the case that Abraham's grandson is the devil. We have contrasted Abraham's righteousness and general characteristic of fair dealing with Israel's self-interest. Israel's birth name *He Grasps the Heel* would go on to become a Hebrew idiom meaning *he deceives*, and this name is well suited to the father of lies. *Satan* means *adversary*. *Israel* itself means *he fights against God* or at best *he struggles with God*. Keeping in mind that the Hebrews' language at the time of Abraham is thought to have had only a few thousand words in it, it is likely that the words meaning *he struggles with God* would not have been different from those meaning *he fights against God*. Similarly, God's proclamation that the serpent will "strike his heel" would have foretold Satan's birth name: *He Grasps the Heel*. Eventually, we were able to show that the two accounts of David's census can be reconciled only if Israel is Satan. This was the capstone on a character study showing that Abraham's most famous grandson was no good person. To the effect that it is said that the greatest trick the devil ever pulled was to convince the world of his nonexistence, very many Abrahamic peoples today are convinced that Israel is God's favorite person. The Ishmaelites whose religion Islam now covers almost two billion people have not much fallen under this delusion, but the Christian religions including Paulites who call themselves Christians cover almost three billion people. A great number of them have an inaccurate perception of Israel's piety. In this section, we will examine a likely motivator for his great impiety.

> ## Genesis 32:9-12 (NIV)
>
> **9** Then Jacob prayed, "O God of my father Abraham, God of my father Isaac, Lord, you who said to me, 'Go back to your country and your relatives, and I will make you prosper,' **10** I am unworthy of all the kindness and faithfulness you have shown your servant. I had only my staff when I crossed this Jordan, but now I have become two camps. **11** Save me, I pray, from the hand of my brother Esau, for I am afraid he will come and attack me, and also the mothers with their children. **12** But you have said, 'I will surely make you prosper and will make your descendants like the sand of the sea, which cannot be counted.'"

Returning home after coming under the bad graces of Laban's family, Satan became fearful when he learned that his brother Esau was coming to meet him with 400 men.[119] At that time, he prayed the prayer recorded in Genesis 32. After repeating his account of God's command to return to Beersheba from Paddan Aram, Satan called himself unworthy, and we will take the conclusion of the prayer in verse 12 as the philosophical predicate underlying his eventual rebellion against God. More or less, we take Satan's thinking to be, "I don't think there's any crime for which you would harshly punish me, Lord, because you have already promised the land to my children, and you have already promised to increase my descendants beyond number." Satan, the self-interested deceiver, determines that if God has already promised to make a great nation of him, then there is nothing he can do which would result in God taking that away.

Satan's grand insight was to see that he and his descendants could engage in any manner of evil, and God would be forced to abide it. While he already had this frame of thinking in mind on the far side of the Jabbok, at some later time he may have learned of the exact mechanism by which God would be forced to protect his own ancestors at any cost. Because they are the tribe of God's ancestors, the Israelites—the children of Satan—are God's chosen people. There is no manner of evil in which they can engage without knowing that God cannot destroy them, no matter how great their sin. God must protect his own ancestors if he is to win the final victory at the end of the age. As we have supposed: the work of ages is to bring the good seed forward to harvest time. This requires the preservation of God's bloodline.

Malachi 3:6 (NIV)

6 "I the Lord do not change. So you, the descendants of Jacob, are not destroyed.["]

121

In Malachi 3, the Lord explains that the descendants of Jacob are not destroyed, or *cannot be destroyed*, because the Lord himself does not change. Satan likely would have learned the nature of this fine print written into the history of the universe while he was *roaming throughout the earth* and *going back and forth on it.*[120] Seeing the structure of the line God had stretched across time, Satan may have thought that he could still preserve that line with himself in the seat of ultimate victory because he and God were from the same line. Here, the problem of Satan is distinguished from the problem of the false Gods whose efforts would have been doomed to failure being rooted in something other than the true vine of life: God's true timeline. At the time when the Living God walks upon the Earth, however, almost none of the contemporary Israelites will be his ancestors. The immutable protection will expire. In this way, God's many promises to punish the children for the sins of their ancestors[121] contextualize a different sort of choosing for the Israelites than is usually understood.

Often it is said that Satan was a high ranking angel in heaven before his fall though this is not exactly recorded in the Bible.[122] Still, the present context for Israel as a time agent who saw his own immutable place in the scheme of things and then sought to raise himself above the Lord is well consistent with the accepted context for Satan's backstory. Once in the time machine, having entered under who knows what kind of circumstances, Satan would have sought to defraud his descendant the Lord in the manner which was usual for him. All the while, Satan would have had it on his mind, "There is nothing I can do for which God will take away the blessings that have already been promised to me."

Notes

[119]Genesis 32:6-8.

[120]Job 1:7.

[121]E.g.: Exodus 20:5, Deuteronomy 23:3-4, Psalm 137:9, Isaiah 14:21, Hosea 13:16, etc.

[122]Isaiah 14:12-15 and Ezekiel 28:12-19 are said to motivate this context for Satan.

15. The History of the Israelites

As God had promised Abraham, Jacob's descendants became slaves in Egypt.[123] Perhaps these centuries of slavery were given in retribution for Israel's crimes. God
eventually sent Moses with ten plagues and an appeal to
Pharaoh to let the Israelites go.[124] Until God killed all of
Egypt's firstborn children in the tenth plague, Pharaoh
was unmoved.[125] Along the way, Pharaoh's *magicians*
told him they could replicate some of the Lord's plagues.
Most interestingly, Pharaoh's magicians could make frogs
but not gnats.[126] This might mean that micro-mechanical
technology was available in Pharaoh's court, but that
they had no mastery of over the far more advanced nano-
mechanics. If it would have been something as plain as
the magicians making frogs by growing tadpoles, then
seemingly gnats would have been easier to farm.

The Israelites' holiest holiday, Passover, commemo-
rates the tenth plague in which God killed the firstborn
among the Egyptians while *passing over* the firstborn
Israelites living in Egypt. It is often lost on those of
the Paulite tradition that Jesus' multiply recorded cel-
ebrations of the Passover were in celebration of God's
massacre of very many Egyptian children.[127] Upon the
massacre, Pharaoh let Moses' people go[128] but then gave
pursuit when he had second thoughts.[129]

Exodus 14:13-31 (NIV)

13 Moses answered the people, "Do not be afraid. Stand firm and you will see the deliverance the Lord will bring you today. The Egyptians you see today you will never see again. 14 The Lord will fight for you; you need only to be still."

15 Then the Lord said to Moses, "Why are you crying out to me? Tell the Israelites to move on. 16 Raise your staff and stretch out your hand over the sea to divide the water so that the Israelites can go through the sea on dry ground. 17 I will harden the hearts of the Egyptians so that they will go in after them. And I will gain glory through Pharaoh and all his army, through his chariots and his horsemen. 18 The Egyptians will know that I am the Lord when I gain glory through Pharaoh, his chariots and his horsemen."

19 Then the angel of God, who had been traveling in front of Israel's army, withdrew and went behind them. The pillar of cloud also moved from in front and stood behind them, 20 coming between the armies of Egypt and Israel. Throughout the night the cloud brought darkness to the one side and light to the other side; so neither went near the other all night long.

21 Then Moses stretched out his hand over the sea, and all that night the Lord drove the sea back with a strong east wind and turned it into

dry land. The waters were divided, 22 and the Israelites went through the sea on dry ground, with a wall of water on their right and on their left.

23 The Egyptians pursued them, and all Pharaoh's horses and chariots and horsemen followed them into the sea. 24 During the last watch of the night the Lord looked down from the pillar of fire and cloud at the Egyptian army and threw it into confusion. 25 He jammed the wheels of their chariots so that they had difficulty driving. And the Egyptians said, "Let's get away from the Israelites! The Lord is fighting for them against Egypt."

26 Then the Lord said to Moses, "Stretch out your hand over the sea so that the waters may flow back over the Egyptians and their chariots and horsemen." 27 Moses stretched out his hand over the sea, and at daybreak the sea went back to its place. The Egyptians were fleeing toward it, and the Lord swept them into the sea. 28 The water flowed back and covered the chariots and horsemen—the entire army of Pharaoh that had followed the Israelites into the sea. Not one of them survived.

29 But the Israelites went through the sea on dry ground, with a wall of water on their right and on their left. 30 That day the Lord saved Israel

> from the hands of the Egyptians, and Israel saw the Egyptians lying dead on the shore. **31** And when the Israelites saw the mighty hand of the Lord displayed against the Egyptians, the people feared the Lord and put their trust in him and in Moses his servant.

God parted the Red Sea, and the pursuing army was swallowed up behind them. As in the case of the talking serpent, the parting of the water is difficult to fathom. Sometimes theologians speculate that wind may have pushed the entire sea away at some tidal equinox, both moving the water and drying the mud of the seabed. On the other hand, if the *waters* and *dry ground* refer to *the past* and *the present*, then God destroyed Pharaoh's army by parting Pharaoh's timeline from the Israelites'. The passage on dry ground promised in verse 16 is evocative of the time bubble interpretation for Noah's ark. In verse 25, the Lord jammed the wheels of Pharaoh's chariots, so, to the extent that Pharaoh's magicians were able to replicate certain of the Lord's plagues, God may have sabotaged the time machines with which the Egyptians gave pursuit. God killed them by their malfunctioning time machines without unleashing time weapons directly, as he had sworn never again to do.[130]

Unbelievers sometimes cite a lack of any archaeological evidence of a mass migration out of Egypt around 1500 BC. Such evidence may have been washed away in the waters of time. There exists a well known discrepancy of more than 100 years between the Jewish calendar and the accepted archaeological calendar,[131] and that could be due to time travel during the migrations of the Israelites. Such time travel would follow in the fashion of God's agents who bring word to and from the future without violating God's prohibition on temporal weaponry.

The Israelites wandered for many years. They almost ran out of water at one point but were saved when a fountain fortuitously sprung from a stone.[132] There is a magical interpretation by which water might spring from a stone, but, more likely, God used his time machine to construct an underground reservoir for Moses' camp where they would have died of dehydration. Eventually, Moses died before the Israelites entered the Promised Land. His successor was Joshua.[133]

Joshua 1:16-18 (KJV)

16 And they answered Joshua, saying, All that thou commandest us we will do, and whithersoever thou sendest us, we will go. **17** According as we hearkened unto Moses in all things, so will we hearken unto thee: only the Lord thy God be with thee, as he was with Moses. **18** Whosoever he be that doth rebel against thy commandment, and will not hearken unto thy words in all that thou commandest him, he shall be put to death: only be strong and of a good courage.

The people did not keep God's covenant of circumcision in the wilderness, but there was a mass circumcision event before the invasion of the Promised Land began.[134] While they were still in the wilderness, God's hand was against the generation of Israel that had lived in Egypt.[135] If God's omnipotence was magical in nature, then he might have snapped his fingers and made that generation disappear. As it was, the people wandered until almost all of the men from the elder generation were dead. God's omnipotence is demonstrated by the ability of the Holy Spirit to write history, so, in that perspective, the 40 years it took for the generation of fighting men from Egypt to pass away *was* a snap of God's fingers.

While Moses still lived, the Lord instructed the Israelites in the way they ought to make war.

Numbers 33:50-56 (NIV)

50 On the plains of Moab by the Jordan across from Jericho the Lord said to Moses, 51 "Speak to the Israelites and say to them: 'When you cross the Jordan into Canaan, 52 drive out all the inhabitants of the land before you. Destroy all their carved images and their cast idols, and demolish all their high places. 53 Take possession of the land and settle in it, for I have given you the land to possess. 54 Distribute the land

by lot, according to your clans. To a larger group give a larger inheritance, and to a smaller group a smaller one. Whatever falls to them by lot will be theirs. Distribute it according to your ancestral tribes.

55 "'But if you do not drive out the inhabitants of the land, those you allow to remain will become barbs in your eyes and thorns in your sides. They will give you trouble in the land where you will live. **56** And then I will do to you what I plan to do to them.'"

Deuteronomy 20:10-18 (NIV)

10 When you march up to attack a city, make its people an offer of peace. **11** If they accept and open their gates, all the people in it shall be subject to forced labor and shall work for you. **12** If they refuse to make peace and they engage you in battle, lay siege to that city. **13** When the Lord your God delivers it into your hand, put to the sword all the men in it. **14** As for the women, the children, the livestock and everything else in the city, you may take these as plunder for yourselves. And you may use the plunder the Lord your God gives you from your enemies. **15** This is how you are to treat all the cities that are at a distance from you and do not belong to the nations nearby.

16 However, in the cities of the nations the Lord your God is giving you as an inheritance, do not leave alive anything that breathes. 17 Completely destroy them—the Hittites, Amorites, Canaanites, Perizzites, Hivites and Jebusites—as the Lord your God has commanded you. 18 Otherwise, they will teach you to follow all the detestable things they do in worshiping their gods, and you will sin against the Lord your God.

Shortly before the conquest of the land began, God spoke to Joshua.

Joshua 1:7 (KJV)

7 Only be thou strong and very courageous, that thou mayest observe to do according to all the law, which Moses my servant commanded thee: turn not from it to the right hand or to the left, that thou mayest prosper whithersoever thou goest.

In Numbers 33, God told Moses that they were to drive out everyone they would find in the land or else God would do to the Israelites what he was planning to do to the people in the land. Joshua did kill more than 30 kings,[136] but he did not exterminate the Gibeonites or drive them away.[137] Instead, Joshua departed from the law given to Moses when he agreed to let the Gibeonites live among the Israelites under a curse. The Gibeonites become an economic underclass among the Israelites who would carry water and cut wood but were barred from stonecutting work.[138] Joshua also departed from the Lord's command when he spared the prostitute Rahab and her household.[139] Whether it was her virtue or something less than that which compelled her to aid the Israelites against her fellow townsfolk is not written. As Joshua would entreat with the Gibeonites, the spies he dispatched from Shittim promised to deliver her.[140] Joshua honored their promise, and she is later recorded among Jesus' ancestors.[141]

Joshua's first attack in the Promised Land was on the city of Jericho whose walls were destroyed when the Israelites blew their horns.[142] Likely God's agents had set explosives and detonated them at the appointed time. After that, Joshua and the Israelites entered Jericho and killed almost everyone: men and women, adults and children, almost as the Lord had commanded Moses. Rahab and her household were spared. During the time of conquest, the Levitical priests carried the Ark of the Covenant with them. The ark may have been a time machine or some other technological artifact. Following the destruction of Jericho, the Israelites were routed at Ai. God told Joshua that they were defeated because the Israelites had sinned by taking *devoted things* as plunder from Jericho instead of destroying it, its people, and their property.[143] One assumes that *devoted things* were time phones and such that may have interfered with the Ark's time field. After the Israelites relinquished their plunder while not revoking Rahab's safe harbor, Joshua led them on to a fantastic campaign of conquest marred only by Rahab's deliverance and his succumbing to the Gibeonites' trickery. One wonders: how great was the magnitude of Joshua's sin?

Judges, the seventh book of the Bible, fairly well summarizes the full history of the Israelites in its thematic content. Chronologically, it follows the Israelites after the death of Joshua until the Israelites began to ask for a king. God told them that he was their king, and that a king would exploit them. Still, they wanted an earthly king "like the other nations."[144] At God's instruction,[145] Saul was anointed king of Israel by Samuel who is sometimes called the last of the judges and the first of the prophets. During the time of the judges, the Israelites could not go long without turning to evil, forsaking the Lord, and worshiping false gods.[146] Every time they would do so, however, some remnant in the tradition of Abraham rather than Israel was still among them. From that remnant, God would raise up a judge to correct the people's wickedness. The Day of Judgment[147] is a continuation of the tradition established in Judges. God himself is one such judge. The Sovereign Lord God Almighty is the supreme judge of the world.

During the Israelite monarchy, things went well for a time. A temple was built by King Solomon, son of David who was king after Saul.[148] To this day, the megalithic foundation stones of Solomon's temple remain stacked in Jerusalem as evidence that some advanced technology was in place long ago and then lost to history, apparently. As in the earlier history of the Israelites, the monarchy and its people could not go long without forsaking the Lord and turning to false gods. After Solomon died, Jeroboam returned from exile to lead a rebellion against the House of David.[149] At that time, Rehoboam son of Solomon was the sort of unloved, non-beneficent king about which Samuel had warned.[150] The monarchy was divided into northern and southern kingdoms.[151]

1 Kings 12:20-31 (NIV)

20 When all the Israelites heard that Jeroboam had returned, they sent and called him to the assembly and made him king over all Israel. Only the tribe of Judah remained loyal to the house of David.

21 When Rehoboam arrived in Jerusalem, he mustered all Judah and the tribe of Benjamin—a hundred and eighty thousand able young men—to go to war against Israel and to regain the kingdom for Rehoboam son of Solomon.

22 But this word of God came to Shemaiah the man of God: **23** "Say to Rehoboam son of

Solomon king of Judah, to all Judah and Benjamin, and to the rest of the people, 24 'This is what the Lord says: Do not go up to fight against your brothers, the Israelites. Go home, every one of you, for this is my doing.'" So they obeyed the word of the Lord and went home again, as the Lord had ordered.

25 Then Jeroboam fortified Shechem in the hill country of Ephraim and lived there. From there he went out and built up Peniel.

26 Jeroboam thought to himself, "The kingdom will now likely revert to the house of David. 27 If these people go up to offer sacrifices at the temple of the Lord in Jerusalem, they will again give their allegiance to their lord, Rehoboam king of Judah. They will kill me and return to King Rehoboam."

28 After seeking advice, the king made two golden calves. He said to the people, "It is too much for you to go up to Jerusalem. Here are your gods, Israel, who brought you up out of Egypt." 29 One he set up in Bethel, and the other in Dan. 30 And this thing became a sin; the people came to worship the one at Bethel and went as far as Dan to worship the other.

31 Jeroboam built shrines on high places and appointed priests from all sorts of people, even

> though they were not Levites.

The Kingdom of Israel was in the north and the Kingdom of Judah was in the south. The capital of Judah was Jerusalem, and Israel was the kingdom of those who had broken away from the Lord. The following passage tells of the last king of Israel before that kingdom was destroyed. The next following passage tells of the king of Judah at the time of the destruction of the northern kingdom.

2 Kings 17:1-41 (NIV)

1 In the twelfth year of Ahaz king of Judah, Hoshea son of Elah became king of Israel in Samaria, and he reigned nine years. **2** He did evil in the eyes of the Lord, but not like the kings of Israel who preceded him.

3 Shalmaneser king of Assyria came up to attack Hoshea, who had been Shalmaneser's vassal and had paid him tribute. **4** But the king of Assyria discovered that Hoshea was a traitor, for he had sent envoys to So king of Egypt, and he no longer paid tribute to the king of Assyria, as he had done year by year. Therefore Shalmaneser seized him and put him in prison. **5** The king of Assyria invaded the entire land, marched against Samaria and laid siege to it for three years. **6** In the ninth year of Hoshea, the king of Assyria captured Samaria and deported the Israelites to Assyria. He settled them in Halah, in Gozan on the Habor River and in the towns of the Medes.

7 All this took place because the Israelites had sinned against the Lord their God, who had brought them up out of Egypt from under the power of Pharaoh king of Egypt. They worshiped other gods 8 and followed the practices of the nations the Lord had driven out before them, as well as the practices that the kings of Israel had introduced. 9 The Israelites secretly did things against the Lord their God that were not right. From watchtower to fortified city they built themselves high places in all their towns. 10 They set up sacred stones and Asherah poles on every high hill and under every spreading tree. 11 At every high place they burned incense, as the nations whom the Lord had driven out before them had done. They did wicked things that aroused the Lord's anger. 12 They worshiped idols, though the Lord had said, "You shall not do this." 13 The Lord warned Israel and Judah through all his prophets and seers: "Turn from your evil ways. Observe my commands and decrees, in accordance with the entire Law that I commanded your ancestors to obey and that I delivered to you through my servants the prophets."

14 But they would not listen and were as stiff-necked as their ancestors, who did not trust in the Lord their God. **15** They rejected his decrees and the covenant he had made with their ancestors and the statutes he had warned them to keep. They followed worthless idols and themselves became worthless. They imitated the nations around them although the Lord had ordered them, "Do not do as they do."

16 They forsook all the commands of the Lord their God and made for themselves two idols cast in the shape of calves, and an Asherah pole. They bowed down to all the starry hosts, and they worshiped Baal. **17** They sacrificed their sons and daughters in the fire. They practiced divination and sought omens and sold themselves to do evil in the eyes of the Lord, arousing his anger.

18 So the Lord was very angry with Israel and removed them from his presence. Only the tribe of Judah was left, **19** and even Judah did not keep the commands of the Lord their God. They followed the practices Israel had introduced. **20** Therefore the Lord rejected all the people of Israel; he afflicted them and gave them into the hands of plunderers, until he thrust them from his presence.

21 When he tore Israel away from the house of

David, they made Jeroboam son of Nebat their king. Jeroboam enticed Israel away from following the Lord and caused them to commit a great sin. 22 The Israelites persisted in all the sins of Jeroboam and did not turn away from them 23 until the Lord removed them from his presence, as he had warned through all his servants the prophets. So the people of Israel were taken from their homeland into exile in Assyria, and they are still there.

24 The king of Assyria brought people from Babylon, Kuthah, Avva, Hamath and Sepharvaim and settled them in the towns of Samaria to replace the Israelites. They took over Samaria and lived in its towns. 25 When they first lived there, they did not worship the Lord; so he sent lions among them and they killed some of the people. 26 It was reported to the king of Assyria: "The people you deported and resettled in the towns of Samaria do not know what the god of that country requires. He has sent lions among them, which are killing them off, because the people do not know what he requires."

27 Then the king of Assyria gave this order: "Have one of the priests you took captive from Samaria go back to live there and teach the people what the god of the land requires." 28 So one of the priests who had been exiled from Samaria

came to live in Bethel and taught them how to worship the Lord.

29 Nevertheless, each national group made its own gods in the several towns where they settled, and set them up in the shrines the people of Samaria had made at the high places. **30** The people from Babylon made Sukkoth Benoth, those from Kuthah made Nergal, and those from Hamath made Ashima; **31** the Avvites made Nibhaz and Tartak, and the Sepharvites burned their children in the fire as sacrifices to Adrammelek and Anammelek, the gods of Sepharvaim. **32** They worshiped the Lord, but they also appointed all sorts of their own people to officiate for them as priests in the shrines at the high places. **33** They worshiped the Lord, but they also served their own gods in accordance with the customs of the nations from which they had been brought.

34 To this day they persist in their former practices. They neither worship the Lord nor adhere to the decrees and regulations, the laws and commands that the Lord gave the descendants of Jacob, whom he named Israel. **35** When the Lord made a covenant with the Israelites, he commanded them: "Do not worship any other gods or bow down to them, serve them or sacrifice to them. **36** But the Lord, who brought you up out of Egypt with mighty power and out-stretched arm, is the one you must worship. To him you shall bow down and to him offer sacrifices. 37 You must always be careful to keep the decrees and regulations, the laws and commands he wrote for you. Do not worship other gods. 38 Do not forget the covenant I have made with you, and do not worship other gods. 39 Rather, worship the Lord your God; it is he who will deliver you from the hand of all your enemies."

40 They would not listen, however, but persisted in their former practices. 41 Even while these people were worshiping the Lord, they were serving their idols. To this day their children and grandchildren continue to do as their ancestors did.

2 Kings 18:1-7 (NIV)

1 In the third year of Hoshea son of Elah king of Israel, Hezekiah son of Ahaz king of Judah began to reign. 2 He was twenty-five years old when he became king, and he reigned in Jerusalem twenty-nine years. His mother's name was Abijah daughter of Zechariah. 3 He did what was right in the eyes of the Lord, just as his father David had done. 4 He removed the high places, smashed the sacred stones and cut down the

Asherah poles. He broke into pieces the bronze snake Moses had made, for up to that time the Israelites had been burning incense to it. (It was called Nehushtan.)

5 Hezekiah trusted in the Lord, the God of Israel. There was no one like him among all the kings of Judah, either before him or after him. 6 He held fast to the Lord and did not stop following him; he kept the commands the Lord had given Moses. 7 And the Lord was with him; he was successful in whatever he undertook. He rebelled against the king of Assyria and did not serve him.

When a new country was formed where British Palestine used to be in 1948, the founders of that country named themselves after the northern kingdom, or after the man Satan himself. The cultural inheritance from the namesake Kingdom of Israel is made plain in 1 Kings 12 and 2 Kings 17. Such things are well attributed to those who are the children of Satan more so than they are the ancestors of the Lord.[152] The concluding words of the record of the history of the ancient Kingdom of Israel relate that those people and their children persisted in their wickedness until at least the time of the scribe.[153] Most likely, the same can be said for many of the far removed great-grandchildren that populate the secular state of Israel in the 21st century. The name of Satan is the name they have chosen for themselves, and for good reason. As it was in Judges and earlier, and in 2 Kings 18, many turn to wickedness, but a remnant in the tradition of Abraham always remains. God must get his genetic material through the Israelites, and his cultural inheritance of righteousness must also come to him from Noah and Abraham in the same way. Fortunately, the Israelites are a much larger group than the Israelis who have named their country *Satan.*

Even in Jerusalem, the capitol of the southern Kingdom of Judah where David son of Jesse the Ephraimite was king, where David's son Solomon was king after him, and where Hezekiah and Josiah were eventually kings, things did not go well forever. The descent into chaos, captivity, and destruction is the time of the major prophets: Isaiah, Jeremiah, and Ezekiel. Following the time of Isaiah, the Babylonians looted Solomon's temple.[154] Almost everyone in Jerusalem was taken to Babylon, including Jehoiachin king of Judah. Among those that remained in Jerusalem, Jehoiachin's uncle was made king.[155] Against the advice of the prophet Jeremiah, the new king Zedekiah rebelled against Nebuchadnezzar king of Babylon. Nebuchadnezzar returned, took what little remained in the temple, destroyed the temple, and brought most of the remnant of Judah into captivity in Babylon.[156] He appointed a governor to rule for him in Jerusalem, but one of King David's descendants assassinated him.[157] Around 2600 years ago, the Persians conquered the Babylonians. The captives in Babylon were allowed to return to Judah at that time,[158] but the Israelites were scattered.[159] There was never another king in Jerusalem and never another governor. Instead, a priestly class was over them. It is likely that the books of the prophets written during this time contain the word of the Lord mixed with the lies of the priests falsely using the phrase, "This is what the Lord says." As Satan had told Simeon and Levi from his deathbed, they were scattered, but so were all of the other Israelite tribes, and not for the reason he had said.

The conclusion of the monarchy was that God sent some remnant of the nobility to become captives in Babylon while the remainder of the people were scattered. Many went into Egypt where God promised to destroy them.[160] When the Israelites went into Babylon, they brought with them their scriptures in the form of the books of Moses, the early histories, some of The Book of Isaiah, and other texts. Eventually, those books made it to ancient Greece. The Greek word *biblios* means *little books*, and the origin of this word is found in the little books that the Israelites brought with them into *Babylon*. Today, the book of the Babylonian religion is called the *Bible* for this reason: it is based on the collection of the Israelites' *biblios* which came to Greece through Babylon.

While we do not present a mathematical analysis here, the accounts of the earlier history of the Israelite tribes going to war every few years and losing so many thousands of men in each battle suggest some context beyond the simple written history. The numbers of the generations of the Israelites cannot be easily reconciled with the many accounts of their military engagements.

144

Notes

[123]Genesis 15:13.

[124]Exodus 3-4.

[125]Exodus 7-12.

[126]Exodus 7:11-12, Exodus 7:22, Exodus 8:7.

[127]A dehumanizing proverb among the Paulites and others is, "God is love," but it is written, "God is a man of war." It is written in 1 John 4:8 that God is love, but this must apply to the Spirit of God which is called by God's name. The Spirit of God is the intention which survives to infinity, and that intention is properly called love because God's purpose is to provide a superior place for the generations from the good seed who will come in the future. God's care for their well-being reflects his love for them.

[128]Exodus 12:31-32.

[129]Exodus 14:5-9.

[130]Genesis 8:21-22.

[131]"Missing years (Jewish calendar)," https://en.wikipedia.org/wiki/Missing_years_(Jewish_calendar).

[132]Exodus 17:1-7.

[133]Numbers 27:15-23, Deuteronomy 31:1-8.

[134]Joshua 5:2-8.

[135]Deuteronomy 2:14-15.

[136]Joshua 12:7-34.

[137]Joshua 9:1-14.

[138]Joshua's lack of carefulness in following God's law and his subsequent treaty with the Gibeonites is probably the origin of the modern day cult of Freemasonry. Joshua's so-called curse may have afflicted the Gibeonites with a fear of missing out from stonecutting work such that their remnant among the Israelites evolved a cult dedicated to that purpose. On the other hand, perhaps it is the remnant of Joshua determined to hold the Gibeonites at bay, or to finally enforce the Lord's edict against them. Later, King Saul's efforts to exterminate the remnant of the Gibeonites are cited as the cause of a famine in the land (2 Samuel 21:1), so God may not desire the completion of Joshua's task. This is to be inferred,

however, only up the case for the lying pen of the scribes. Since we have already shown in Section 13 that Satan incited David to take a census that God did not want, this case is not to be discounted out of hand. Satan was active in David's court, and it was not Nathan that brought God's word to David in 2 Samuel 21.

[139] Joshua 6:25.

[140] Joshua 2:12-14.

[141] Matthew 1:5.

[142] Joshua 6:20-21.

[143] Joshua 7:2-12.

[144] 1 Samuel 8:5-22. God's grievance against the Israelites was always their desire to follow the ways of other nations. Asking for a king may be the foremost example.

[145] 1 Samuel 9:17.

[146] Judges 2:10-19, Judges 3:7-14, Judges 4:1, Judges 6:1, Judges 10:6-14, Judges 13:1.

[147] Ecclesiastes 12:13-14, John 12:48, etc.

[148] 1 Kings 6.

[149] 1 Kings 12:15-20.

[150] 1 Samuel 8:10-20.

[151] 1 Kings 12, 2 Chronicles 10.

[152] As time goes by, fewer and fewer of the Israelites are among God's ancestors. When God comes into the world, almost none of the Israelites will be among them. However, all of them will still be the children of Satan.

[153] 2 Kings 17:41.

[154] 2 Chronicles 36:5-7, 2 Kings 24:1.

[155] 2 Chronicles 36:10.

[156] 2 Chronicles 36:15-20.

[157] 2 Kings 25:22-25.

[158] 2 Chronicles 36:20-23.

[159] 2 Kings 25:26.

[160] Jeremiah 44:11-14.

16. Isaiah, Jeremiah, and Ezekiel

Isaiah was a prophet before the Babylonians destroyed Solomon's temple and took the surviving priests and nobles of Judah back to Babylon. Jeremiah was a prophet in Jerusalem both before and after Nebuchadnezzar king of Babylon mounted his campaigns against Jerusalem. Ezekiel was a prophet among the exiles in Babylon. Extensive archaeological evidence confirms that the Babylonians raided Jerusalem around 2700 years ago, but the Jewish calendar records these events as having taken place around 2500 years ago. We suggest that the large discrepancy in the chronology is related to time travel. While the structure of the three major prophets' books varies quite a bit from one to another, each contains an account of commission into prophecy.

Isaiah 6:1-13 (NIV)

1 In the year that King Uzziah died, I saw the Lord, high and exalted, seated on a throne; and the train of his robe filled the temple. 2 Above him were seraphim, each with six wings: With two wings they covered their faces, with two they covered their feet, and with two they were flying. 3 And they were calling to one another:

"Holy, holy, holy is the Lord Almighty;
the whole earth is full of his glory."

147

4 At the sound of their voices the doorposts and thresholds shook and the temple was filled with smoke.

5 "Woe to me!" I cried. "I am ruined! For I am a man of unclean lips, and I live among a people of unclean lips, and my eyes have seen the King, the Lord Almighty."

6 Then one of the seraphim flew to me with a live coal in his hand, which he had taken with tongs from the altar. 7 With it he touched my mouth and said, "See, this has touched your lips; your guilt is taken away and your sin atoned for."

8 Then I heard the voice of the Lord saying, "Whom shall I send? And who will go for us?"

And I said, "Here am I. Send me!"

9 He said, "Go and tell this people:

"'Be ever hearing, but never understanding;
  be ever seeing, but never perceiving.'
10 Make the heart of this people calloused;
    make their ears dull
    and close their eyes.
  Otherwise they might see with their eyes,
    hear with their ears,
    understand with their hearts,
  and turn and be healed."

11 Then I said, "For how long, Lord?"

And he answered:

> "Until the cities lie ruined
> and without inhabitant,
> until the houses are left deserted
> and the fields ruined and ravaged,
> 12 until the Lord has sent everyone far away
> and the land is utterly forsaken.
> 13 And though a tenth remains in the land,
> it will again be laid waste.
> But as the terebinth and oak
> leave stumps when they are cut down,
> so the holy seed will be the stump in the
> land."

Verses nine and ten suggest that Isaiah was commissioned sometime after God had decided to leave the weeds until the time of the harvest. He does not want the wicked to be healed. These verses speak to a theme of contradiction throughout the prophets. Sometimes God says, "I'm going to destroy you." Sometimes he says, "If you stop doing what is evil in my sight, then I will not destroy you." To make sense of these things, we will call attention to the character of the prophetic language which is at least superficially contradictory. Overall, the theme is as stated above. There are few unconditional promises of redemption, but there are many unconditional promises of destruction. There is little material with which to frame a theme of contradiction between God's unconditional promises of salvation and his conditional threats of destruction if the Israelites should continue in their wickedness (which is what they did, according to the Bible.) God's message in the three major prophets leans toward destruction. His words to Isaiah in verses nine and ten are understood to mean, "I have already decided to burn the Israelites in the fire at the end of the age, so it is better that they do not understand and be healed only to go into the fire at harvest time anyways."

Jeremiah 1:4-8 (KJV)

4 Then the word of the Lord came unto me, saying, 5 Before I formed thee in the belly I knew thee; and before thou camest forth out of the womb I sanctified thee, and I ordained thee a prophet unto the nations. 6 Then said I, Ah, Lord God! behold, I cannot speak: for I am a child.

7 But the Lord said unto me, Say not, I am a child: for thou shalt go to all that I shall send thee, and whatsoever I command thee thou shalt speak. 8 Be not afraid of their faces: for I am with thee to deliver thee, saith the Lord.

The commission of Jeremiah contains a verse that is taken out of context possibly more than any other: verse five. Although God speaks these words to Jeremiah, many modernists interpret *thee* to be the reader of the Bible so that God is said to tell the reader that he knows *them* in the way that he knew Jeremiah: the last prophet to bring God's word to an Israelite king in Jerusalem. Unlike Isaiah and Ezekiel, the commission of Jeremiah does not contain an account of the appearance of a strange vehicle and/or creature. The first chapter of Ezekiel is a long and vivid account of such an appearance. The direct commissioning appears in the second chapter.

Ezekiel 2:1-10 (NIV)

1 He said to me, "Son of man, stand up on your feet and I will speak to you." 2 As he spoke, the Spirit came into me and raised me to my feet, and I heard him speaking to me.

3 He said: "Son of man, I am sending you to the Israelites, to a rebellious nation that has rebelled against me; they and their ancestors have been in revolt against me to this very day. 4 The people to whom I am sending you are obstinate and stubborn. Say to them, 'This is what the Sovereign Lord says.' 5 And whether they listen or fail to listen—for they are a rebellious people—they will know that a prophet has been among them. 6 And you, son of man, do not be

afraid of them or their words. Do not be afraid, though briers and thorns are all around you and you live among scorpions. Do not be afraid of what they say or be terrified by them, though they are a rebellious people. 7 You must speak my words to them, whether they listen or fail to listen, for they are rebellious. 8 But you, son of man, listen to what I say to you. Do not rebel like that rebellious people; open your mouth and eat what I give you."

9 Then I looked, and I saw a hand stretched out to me. In it was a scroll, 10 which he unrolled before me. On both sides of it were written words of lament and mourning and woe.

The language in verse five contrasts the language in Isaiah's commission. For Ezekiel, God shows indifference to whether or not the exiles will listen. For Isaiah, God said it was better for them not to listen. In the opinion of this writer, this suggests that God commissioned Ezekiel before Isaiah.

A major theme in the first chapter of Isaiah was the rebelliousness of the Israelite nation.[161] This is the major theme in the first half of Ezekiel as well.[162] For the time travel interpretation, the Israelites are the base of power for Satan's rebellion against God, and they may tend to prefer him overtly as much as they may have been misled by him. To characterize their rebelliousness as something more than the service to false gods which is usually assumed, note that the Lord is the God of all mankind.[163] Many of the Jewish Israelite tradition possess a favoritism to think of non-Israelites as mere livestock on par with the flocks of Jacob. Particularly, God promised to make Abraham into the father of many nations.[164] His angel promised Hagar that her descendants would become uncountably many[165] long before Ishmael's nephew Jacob was born. God often promises destruction to the Israelites and the Edomite nation of Abraham's other grandson Esau,[166] but the Ishmaelites fare very well in the telling of God's wrath. God does not have a single word of damnation for the Ishmaelites anywhere in the Bible. Therefore, certain thinking to the effect that God loves Jewish and Christian Israelites (or only the Jewish ones) but not Islamic Ishmaelites must reflect the wiles of the devil and his continuing rebellion. Such thinking has no basis in the scripture.[167] Discord between the Judeo-Christian and Islamic worlds is political in nature, not religious, excepting the case of an ancient enmity between Sarah, Hagar, and their children.[168]

Among the major prophets, Ezekiel is the most coherent narrative of interaction between God and his prophet, so we will start there and then examine Jeremiah. Then we will briefly discuss The Book of Isaiah whose extensive poetic stanzas are not readily amenable to exact analysis. When we considered Isaiah 14 in Section 13, we suggested that the original scroll had been spliced. In the present section, we will make the case that the books of all three major prophets were spliced or edited by the priests and scribes who came after the prophets and the collapse of the monarchy. Almost all scholars agree that this splicing happened. A post-monarchic group of editors known as the Deuteronomists[169] is cited in many Biblical analyses, but here we will exceed the usual analysis to focus on possible bad faith editing. The distinct, splice-likely sections of Ezekiel begin at chapters one, 25, 33, and 40. We will refer to chapters one through 24 as the primary account of Ezekiel.

Ezekiel was a prophet among the exiles. After him, there was never another king of Judah enthroned in Jerusalem. When the Babylonian captivity ended, the priests were a plutocratic oligarchy over the Israelites. Much of what is called the Hebrew Bible today was assembled during the time of the post-monarchic priesthood which followed the many centuries of the Israelites' rebellion. While the Word of God comes to Ezekiel to be passed on to the Israelites in chapters one through 24, everything in chapters 25 through 32 is directed toward foreign nations. It may be that the prophecies of Ezekiel were sectioned so that the material directed to foreign nations was given its own section. On the other hand, after the kingdoms of Israel and Judah were no more, it may have been politically expedient for the priests to be able to say to the kings of the neighboring nations, "Look! The Lord has words for you as well!" Separate from the other foreign prophecy, chapter 36 is an outlier directed toward the Edomites.

The theme of the first 24 chapters of Ezekiel is that the rebellious Israelites will know that God is the Lord when he brings disaster on them.[170]

Ezekiel 5:8-17 (NIV)

8 "Therefore this is what the Sovereign Lord says: I myself am against you, Jerusalem, and I will inflict punishment on you in the sight of the nations. 9 Because of all your detestable idols, I will do to you what I have never done before and will never do again. 10 Therefore in your midst parents will eat their children, and children will eat their parents. I will inflict punishment on you and will scatter all your survivors to the winds. 11 Therefore as surely as I live, declares the Sovereign Lord, because you have defiled my sanctuary with all your vile images and detestable practices, I myself will shave you; I will not look on you with pity or spare you. 12 A third of your people will die of the plague or perish by famine inside you; a third will fall by the sword outside your walls; and a third I will scatter to the winds and pursue with drawn sword.

13 "Then my anger will cease and my wrath against them will subside, and I will be avenged. And when I have spent my wrath on them, they will know that I the Lord have spoken in my zeal.

14 "I will make you a ruin and a reproach among the nations around you, in the sight of all who

pass by. **15** You will be a reproach and a taunt, a warning and an object of horror to the nations around you when I inflict punishment on you in anger and in wrath and with stinging rebuke. I the Lord have spoken. **16** When I shoot at you with my deadly and destructive arrows of famine, I will shoot to destroy you. I will bring more and more famine upon you and cut off your supply of food. **17** I will send famine and wild beasts against you, and they will leave you childless. Plague and bloodshed will sweep through you, and I will bring the sword against you. I the Lord have spoken."

These verses from Ezekiel 5 are well representative of the content in the first 24 chapters. Only once in those chapters does Ezekiel say that something good will happen, and then the people will know that the Lord has acted.

Ezekiel 16:59-63 (NIV)

59 "'This is what the Sovereign Lord says: I will deal with you as you deserve, because you have despised my oath by breaking the covenant. **60** Yet I will remember the covenant I made with you in the days of your youth, and I will establish an everlasting covenant with you. **61** Then you will remember your ways and be ashamed when you receive your sisters, both those who are older than you and those who are younger. I will give them to you as daughters, but not on the basis of my covenant with you. **62** So I will establish my covenant with you, and you will know that I am the Lord. **63** Then, when I make atonement for you for all you have done, you will remember and be ashamed and never again open your mouth because of your humiliation, declares the Sovereign Lord.'"

The context of this outlying prophecy in the primary account of Ezekiel is very strange. If the written things are not to be on the basis of the covenant, as in verse 61, then what is the basis? Ezekiel 15, the previous chapter, is so short that one wonders if part of the original scroll was removed. The second chapter of Ezekiel describing the prophet's commission is also very short. However, the outlying prophecy found in Ezekiel 16 appears at the end of what is by far Ezekiel's longest chapter. One wonders if this single instance of knowing that God is the Lord for some reason other than destruction was spliced onto the end of chapter 16 after the fact.

Ezekiel's vision of the valley of dry bones, to which we will return when examining Jesus' resurrection in Section 20, shows that nothing is too hard for the Lord. This message appears in Jeremiah as well.[171]

Ezekiel 37:1-9 (NIV)

1 The hand of the Lord was on me, and he brought me out by the Spirit of the Lord and set me in the middle of a valley; it was full of bones. 2 He led me back and forth among them, and I saw a great many bones on the floor of the valley, bones that were very dry. 3 He asked me, "Son of man, can these bones live?"

I said, "Sovereign Lord, you alone know."

4 Then he said to me, "Prophesy to these bones and say to them, 'Dry bones, hear the word of the Lord! 5 This is what the Sovereign Lord says to these bones: I will make breath enter you, and you will come to life. 6 I will attach tendons to you and make flesh come upon you and cover you with skin; I will put breath in you, and you will come to life. Then you will know that I am the Lord.'"

7 So I prophesied as I was commanded. And as I was prophesying, there was a noise, a rattling sound, and the bones came together, bone to bone. 8 I looked, and tendons and flesh appeared on them and skin covered them, but there was no breath in them.

9 Then he said to me, "Prophesy to the breath; prophesy, son of man, and say to it, 'This is what

> the Sovereign Lord says: Come, breath, from the
> four winds and breathe into these slain, that they
> may live.'"

While the valley of dry bones is a segue into a promise of healing for Israel at odds with the primary account of Ezekiel, the imagery of the healing of the bones is remarkable. Particularly in the time travel interpretation, the reconstruction of the flesh in verses seven and eight speaks to some advanced medical technology. The vision describes the 3D printing of biological tissues as well as could any modern human. If not 3D printing, perhaps God rewound time until flesh was on the bones again. Even if the account was only a parable given to Ezekiel in a vision, the semblance of regrowing the tissues in the manner of modern sci-fi medical technology is uncanny. It gives the account an air of authenticity, in the opinion of this writer. In the primary account of Ezekiel, chapter 15 appears to have been cut short after describing the uselessness of a vine burnt at both ends.[172] To the extent that God's ability to regrow tissue[173] follows logically after the account of the uselessness of a burnt vine, the prophecy of the valley of dry bones may have appeared in Ezekiel 15 before it was removed and later appended in chapter 37. The technological magnificence of the valley of dry bones is well aligned with the similar magnificence described elsewhere in the primary account, but it seems out of place between chapters 33 and 39, in the opinion of this writer.

JONATHAN W. TOOKER

The second section of Ezekiel gives prophecy for foreigners. The first chapter of the third section, chapter 33, contains an almost verbatim repetition[174] of Ezekiel's earlier call to be a watchman.[175] The tone of the prophecy of the third section is at odds with that in the first section, to say the least. After the repetition of Ezekiel's call, almost every time the Israelites will know that the Lord has acted, the sign will be that the Lord has brought blessings on them.[176] This is the polar opposite of the prophecy in the primary account. The main exceptions in the third part are that twice foreigners will know that the Lord has acted when he destroys foreign nations.[177] Thus, even the exceptions support the theme of an alleged reversal of God's attitude. The third and final exception in this part of Ezekiel follows the repetition of the call to be a watchman.[178] In that instance, the Israelites will know that the Lord has acted because he has laid waste to Jerusalem. This single instance of, "You will know that the Lord has acted when he brings disaster on the Israelites," refers to an event that had already happened and was in the very recent memory of the intended audience for the re-prophesied third section: the exiles in Babylon or their near descendants. In the opinion of this writer, Ezekiel 33 through 39 contains a dishonest rewrite of the original account of Ezekiel. The valley of dry bones may have been repurposed to give the rewrite enhanced credibility. Perhaps the rewrite came from another time.

Some of the material in the rewrite is accurate. The account of Ezekiel's call to be a watchman is the same in the third and thirty-third chapters. The thematic difference between the original chapters of Ezekiel and those which we suggest were added later is that God's promises of destruction give way to promises of redemption. All of the, "God will destroy you," language is replaced with, "Even though you are evil, God will bless you." We have previously suggested that the hand of the devil worked in history to pollute God's word, so it is notable that the crux of the contradiction between the earlier and later prophecy is exactly what we have called the Satanic thesis in Section 14. In the beginning of Ezekiel, God curses the Israelites and damns them for their rebelliousness. God tells them that they will know he is the Lord when he brings disaster on them. In the rewrite following the restatement of Ezekiel's call, they will know that the Lord has acted when he makes good on the Satanic thesis. Most notably, there is not one mention of the rebelliousness of the Israelites following the restatement of Ezekiel's call. One imagines that the rebels preferred the version without that language.

Regarding contradictory prophecies, the Lord says that if a prophecy is not fulfilled, that is a sign that the words of the prophecy did not come from the Lord.[179]

Ezekiel 36:33-36 (NIV)

33 "'This is what the Sovereign Lord says: On the day I cleanse you from all your sins, I will resettle your towns, and the ruins will be re-

> built. **34** The desolate land will be cultivated
> instead of lying desolate in the sight of all who
> pass through it. **35** They will say, "This land
> that was laid waste has become like the garden of
> Eden; the cities that were lying in ruins, desolate
> and destroyed, are now fortified and inhabited."
> **36** Then the nations around you that remain will
> know that I the Lord have rebuilt what was de-
> stroyed and have replanted what was desolate. I
> the Lord have spoken, and I will do it.'[''']

When the Persians conquered the Babylonians, the captives were allowed to go home, but the Israelites were scattered among the nations. Only two tribes had remained in Judah after Israel was absorbed into Assyria. Even then, the captives taken to Babylon did not number very many to begin with. Jerusalem remains a ruin to this day. Its walls and ruins were never rebuilt. Its structures are made from concrete which crumbles in a few decades. Unlike the Garden of Eden, Judah is riddled with road barriers, crude fences, and concertina wire. The Satanists in the secular state of Israel may claim that the prophecy of Ezekiel 36 is yet to be fulfilled, even in the present day, but Ezekiel was very clear that his prophecies did not regard the distant future.[180]

Ezekiel 11:17 (NIV)

17 "Therefore say: 'This is what the Sovereign Lord says: I will gather you from the nations and bring you back from the countries where you have been scattered, and I will give you back the land of Israel again.'["]

The children of Satan enforcing the present-day military occupation of British Palestine will claim that God has given them the right in Ezekiel 11, but this is not so.

Ezekiel 12:26-28 (NIV)

26 The word of the Lord came to me: 27 "Son of man, the Israelites are saying, 'The vision he sees is for many years from now, and he prophesies about the distant future.'

28 "Therefore say to them, 'This is what the Sovereign Lord says: None of my words will be delayed any longer; whatever I say will be fulfilled, declares the Sovereign Lord.'"

The promise of the return to the land was fulfilled when Persia conquered Babylon around 540 BC: hardly beyond the lifetime of the first generation exiles. Around 200 years later, Alexander the Great conquered the Promised Land. A few centuries later, the Romans showed up, and the rest is history. More likely than that it fulfills a prophecy of Ezekiel, the secular state of Israel fulfills a vision revealed to John of Patmos.

Revelation 20:1-3 (NIV)

1 And I saw an angel coming down out of heaven, having the key to the Abyss and holding in his hand a great chain. 2 He seized the dragon, that ancient serpent, who is the devil, or Satan, and bound him for a thousand years. 3 He threw him into the Abyss, and locked and sealed it over him, to keep him from deceiving the nations anymore until the thousand years were ended. After that, he must be set free for a short time.

In this way, the Kingdom of Israel was destroyed. Then the kingdom of the remnant of the Israelites in Judah was destroyed. Then time on the order of 1,000 years passed. Now there is a country in the world named *Satan* once again. Ezekiel prophesied that the crown of David would not be restored until the coming of him to whom it rightfully belongs.[181] The coming of this person was also referenced by Satan on his deathbed.[182] As it remains to this day, those people have no king. The non-constitutional parliamentary system of the secular state of *Satan* has no king and neither do any of the Israelites in the diaspora.[183]

Following what appears to be a partial rewrite of the

original account of Ezekiel, the final eight chapters describe the priesthood and a large temple. The attention to detail regarding what material wealth is to be brought to the priests[184] is evocative of similar language in Leviticus.[185] Where we have suggested that the priests did not do justice to the Lord's word following the destruction of the first temple, the issue of the Levites only counting themselves in one of the two original censuses[186] raises the idea that perhaps the priests were acting not selflessly even before the monarchic period. During the monarchy, we found that Satan incited David to take a census of the Israelites. Satan would have had to collect census data if he was going to tell his children what would become of their tribes.[187] Even with a time machine, telling the fortunes of the tribes of Israel would require census data. Furthermore, the prominent census issue in the history of the Israelites should pertain to the issue of child sacrifice. By taking the census, one's ability to alter later populations by killing children in earlier populations is enhanced.

Jeremiah is less poetic than Isaiah but still more so than Ezekiel who was commissioned as a prophet in Babylon while Jeremiah was a prophet in Jerusalem. There, Jeremiah suffered greatly for his service to the Lord. He is hated and mistreated for his prophecy against Judah. He is beaten, put in stocks, imprisoned, and thrown into a sewer to die.[188] Beyond that, the wickedness in Jerusalem during the time of the prophets is told in Jeremiah's many damnations of their child sacrifice and service to persons such as Moloch.[189]

Deuteronomy 12:31-32 (NIV)

31 You must not worship the Lord your God in their way, because in worshiping their gods, they do all kinds of detestable things the Lord hates. They even burn their sons and daughters in the fire as sacrifices to their gods.

32 See that you do all I command you; do not add to it or take away from it.

God's hatred for child sacrifice must be reconciled with his command for Abraham to kill Isaac. While we have suggested that it was not possible for God to prevent Satan's rebellion in this way due to a paradox in his genetic ancestry, Abraham being compelled to sacrifice his son might have spoiled the heritage of righteousness which comes to the Lord from Noah and Abraham. Namely, it was not sufficient for the work of ages only for God to be born. God's victory at the end of all things is derived from the righteousness of his intentions. Though God sent Abraham to offer Isaac as a burnt offering, possibly in the heat of the melee of his battle with the devil, possibly as a last ditch attempt because he hated Satan more than he hated child sacrifice, God did not want Abraham to do it in the end. A ram was burnt instead.[190]

In Jeremiah, the Lord goes on to reiterate verse 32's ancillary concern about adding to or taking away from the record of God's word.

Jeremiah 8:8-9 (NIV)

8 "'How can you say, "We are wise,
      for we have the law of the Lord,"
   when actually the lying pen of the scribes
      has handled it falsely?
9 The wise will be put to shame;
      they will be dismayed and trapped.
   Since they have rejected the word of the
   Lord,
      what kind of wisdom do they have?

Jeremiah 8 cites the problem of the lying pen of the scribes to which we have made extensive reference in our treatment of Ezekiel, and in our study of Satan. God himself referenced this grave problem in Deuteronomy 12 long before Jeremiah prophesied against it. As earlier, we suggest that the balance between, "I will destroy you," and, "If you repent, then maybe I won't destroy you," gives the theme of God's prophecy differently than would be given by a majority of statements of certain redemption balanced against some statements of conditional destruction. Mostly, the message is that the Lord is going to burn the weeds in the fire. Relating to the coming harvest, we take the following prophecy of the end of days to refer to a time when Israel's name will go away, and only God's name will remain. It does not appear to be the message in the Bible, in the opinion of this writer, that the name of Israel is one to be glorified.

Zechariah 14:9 (NIV)

9 The Lord will be king over the whole earth. On that day there will be one Lord, and his name the only name.

Pertaining to the time travel interpretation, Jeremiah 33 references God's covenant with the day and night: the words God spoke in this heart following the destruction of the Earth under his flood.[191] In Section 8, God's words were taken to reference a promise of an uninterrupted flow of time forever, and this theme is continued during the time of the prophets.

Jeremiah 33:19-26 (NIV)

19 The word of the Lord came to Jeremiah: **20** "This is what the Lord says: 'If you can break my covenant with the day and my covenant with the night, so that day and night no longer come at their appointed time, **21** then my covenant with David my servant—and my covenant with the Levites who are priests ministering before me— can be broken and David will no longer have a descendant to reign on his throne. **22** I will make the descendants of David my servant and the Levites who minister before me as countless as the stars in the sky and as measureless as the sand on the seashore.'"

23 The word of the Lord came to Jeremiah: **24** "Have you not noticed that these people are saying, 'The Lord has rejected the two kingdoms he chose'? So they despise my people and no longer regard them as a nation. **25** This is what the Lord says: 'If I have not made my covenant with day and night and established the laws of heaven and earth, **26** then I will reject the descendants of Jacob and David my servant and will not choose one of his sons to rule over the descendants of Abraham, Isaac and Jacob. For I will restore their fortunes and have compassion on them.'"

God explains that in order to break his covenant with Abraham's descendants, he would have to disrupt time to some high degree to get another history written. The other covenants counted in the previous sections were that the descendants of Abraham, Isaac, and Jacob would become more numerous than the stars, that David's heir would always be king, and that the Levites would always be the Lord's priests. Following the collapse of the Israelite monarchy, David's heir has become a king without a crown. As Ezekiel prophesied, the Israelite crown will not be restored until the coming of the Messiah.[192] In verse 22, God promised that David and Levi are also on the bloodline of the ancestors of innumerable descendants. Should all the other Israelites perish, God's covenants will be fulfilled if the Lord himself is from the lines of Levi and David jointly, and if his own descendants go on to become more numerous than the stars. All of God's descendants will be Israel's descendants, and Abraham's. Should all of the other children of Satan perish, the covenants will be fulfilled. In this way, we offer a further reconciliation between the many prophetic promises of destruction and redemption. Redemption can come at the end through God alone. The covenant with the Israelites would be fulfilled through the one they rebelled against. At minimum, the 144,000 Israelites sealed in Revelation suggest that most will not be redeemed.[193]

When God references his covenant with the day and night in Jeremiah, he mentions a necessity for disrupting time to some high degree if he were to change what has been foretold. In the following from Isaiah 38, God shows by a demonstration to King Hezekiah that he is still able under the terms of his covenant to disrupt time to some degree. Perhaps God moved Hezekiah through time and not the world around him so that time itself was not disrupted at all. Perhaps God's flood came after God had already healed Hezekiah. In either case, and while the flood would seem to precede the history of the flood's survivors, the mind of God is unknowable.

Isaiah 38:1-8 (NIV)

1 In those days Hezekiah became ill and was at the point of death. The prophet Isaiah son of Amoz went to him and said, "This is what the Lord says: Put your house in order, because you are going to die; you will not recover."

2 Hezekiah turned his face to the wall and prayed to the Lord, 3 "Remember, Lord, how I have walked before you faithfully and with whole-hearted devotion and have done what is good in your eyes." And Hezekiah wept bitterly.

4 Then the word of the Lord came to Isaiah: 5 "Go and tell Hezekiah, 'This is what the Lord, the God of your father David, says: I have heard your prayer and seen your tears; I will add fifteen years to your life. 6 And I will deliver you and this city from the hand of the king of Assyria. I will defend this city.

7 "'This is the Lord's sign to you that the Lord will do what he has promised: 8 I will make the shadow cast by the sun go back the ten steps it has gone down on the stairway of Ahaz.'" So the sunlight went back the ten steps it had gone down.

During the years of Isaiah, God saw that Hezekiah

was going to die. As it is written in 2 Kings 18, Hezekiah was a righteous king, so God rewound time slightly[194] to put him on another timeline where his death would be postponed for 15 years. The account of Pharaoh's fate in the Red Sea[195] also tells that God retains the power to control time even within the terms of his covenant with the night and day. The means by which God acts are described in Jeremiah 18.

Jeremiah 18:1-10 (NIV)

1 This is the word that came to Jeremiah from the Lord: 2 "Go down to the potter's house, and there I will give you my message." 3 So I went down to the potter's house, and I saw him working at the wheel. 4 But the pot he was shaping from the clay was marred in his hands; so the potter formed it into another pot, shaping it as seemed best to him.

5 Then the word of the Lord came to me. 6 He said, "Can I not do with you, Israel, as this potter does?" declares the Lord. "Like clay in the hand of the potter, so are you in my hand, Israel. 7 If at any time I announce that a nation or kingdom is to be uprooted, torn down and destroyed, 8 and if that nation I warned repents of its evil, then I will relent and not inflict on it

> the disaster I had planned. **9** And if at another time I announce that a nation or kingdom is to be built up and planted, **10** and if it does evil in my sight and does not obey me, then I will reconsider the good I had intended to do for it.

Regarding the Israelites specifically, the Lord says, "And if at another time I announce that a nation or kingdom is to be built up and planted, and if it does evil in my sight and does not obey me, then I will reconsider the good I had intended to do for it." The Satanic thesis is that God is *not* like the potter.

Aside from the lying pen of the scribes, Jeremiah describes a problem of people claiming to have dreamt that the Lord told them to do something even when the Lord did not.[196] To the extent that Satan told his wives that the Lord's angel told him in a dream to flee from Laban,[197] one wonders if that really happened. It is written that the Lord told him to return to his native land,[198] but Jacob's lie would be a ready explanation for why God fought and injured him at the edge of the river.[199] Perhaps *Jacob* came to mean *he deceives* because he lied about God to his father,[200] and also about God's angel in his dream. A frame of events in which God never told Jacob to return to Beersheba is less complicated than the other suppositions we have given in Sections 11 and 12 regarding why God would have fought and hurt him on his journey home. Was Jacob not going where the Lord had told him to go? Once one begins to question the scripture, there is no limit to the meaning that can be extracted by cherry-picking the verses. What is written, however, is that God himself sent word through Jeremiah that scribes write lies, and other people lie about what the Lord told them.[201] Satan is called the father of lies.[202] Jacob means *he deceives*. Satan lied about God to his father to say that the Lord had given him success in a hunt he never went on. A discrepancy between dialogue attributed jointly to God himself and an angel of God in Jacob's dream[203] suggests that he may have lied about God telling him to leave Laban's camp as well. When an angel spoke to Abraham as Isaac was on the altar of sacrifice, the angel said, "I swear by myself, declares the Lord."[204] In Jacob's account of his dream in Paddan Aram, the angel said, "I am God,"[205] which he was not.

Jehoiakim, wicked king of Judah, eventually burned the scroll containing the prophecy of Jeremiah.[206] Jeremiah then rewrote an expanded version of it.[207] Still, even that was not the end of The Book of Jeremiah. More words were added later. Now we will discuss some similarities between the later chapters in Jeremiah and Ezekiel.

After the main body of Jeremiah's prophecy ends in chapter 26, Jeremiah goes on to name Nebuchadnezzar as God's servant.[208] This is strange considering the damnation of the king of Babylon found in Isaiah 14 and elsewhere. Shortly before the king of Babylon is praised, God is recorded as telling Jeremiah to send word to the same kings[209] that are prophesied to in Ezekiel's second section[210] (between the primary account and the rewrite.)

The second section of Ezekiel contains only two foreign nations not listed in Jeremiah 27: Egypt and Philistia. In the later section of Jeremiah that is devoted to foreign nations, chapters 46 through 51, Egypt and Philistia are the first two nations cited in an apparent completion of the catalog of the Israelites' neighbors. This supports the idea that the post-captivity priesthood added material to its scrolls so that it could report to the more powerful nations in the surrounding lands that the word of the Lord pertains to them as well. Maybe the foreign prophecy was the Lord's word. Maybe it wasn't. When the foreign-only section in Jeremiah gives prophecy for the Moabites and the Ammonites, redemption is promised[211] though scripture in Deuteronomy had already prohibited them from entering into the assembly of the Lord.[212] Deuteronomy forbids it "even unto the tenth generation." This is usually taken to mean that anyone with a male Ammonite or Moabite ancestor going back ten generations is cursed, but maybe it meant that the curse was to last for ten generations from the time of Deuteronomy. If it was the former, then the contradiction in Jeremiah's alleged treatment of the descendants of Lot—Moab and Ammon—can be understood in terms of the lying priests' attempts to curry favor with the nations around them.

Jeremiah 32:17-19 (KJV)

17 Ah Lord God! behold, thou hast made the

> heaven and the earth by thy great power and stretched out arm, and there is nothing too hard for thee: **18** Thou shewest lovingkindness unto thousands, and recompensest the iniquity of the fathers into the bosom of their children after them: the Great, the Mighty God, the Lord of hosts, is his name, **19** Great in counsel, and mighty in work: for thine eyes are open upon all the ways of the sons of men: to give every one according to his ways, and according to the fruit of his doings[.]

God rewards each person as he sees fit, and that includes punishing children for the sins of their ancestors. This is a valuable rod of justice in the time travel context because it allows God to repay as he sees fit *and* at the time of his choosing. In the law God gave to the Israelites for dealing with each other, God commanded them not to punish a man's children for his crimes, but that was for justice among the Israelites, not between God and man.

Deuteronomy 24:16 (NIV)

16 Parents are not to be put to death for their children, nor children put to death for their parents; each will die for their own sin.

Exodus 20:5 (NIV)

5 You shall not bow down to them or worship them; for I, the Lord your God, am a jealous God, punishing the children for the sin of the parents to the third and fourth generation of those who hate me[.]

Deuteronomy 5:9 (NIV)

9 You shall not bow down to them or worship them; for I, the Lord your God, am a jealous God, punishing the children for the sin of the parents to the third and fourth generation of those who hate me[.]

It can hardly be questioned that God punishes children for their ancestors' sins even while this is forbidden for others. Jeremiah and Ezekiel both contain references to an Israelite proverb: when fathers eat sour grapes, it sets their children's teeth on edge.[213] In both places, the scribe foretells that children will no longer be punished for their parents' crimes, and that the proverb will cease to be quoted. Ezekiel does not contextualize the time at which this proverb will fall into disuse, but Jeremiah makes reference to the time of a new covenant.[214] Many of the Paulite tradition take Jeremiah's new covenant

177

to mean that God has chosen to renege on his original covenant with the Israelites, and that, instead, for some reason, we should expect God not to renege on a new covenant. More reasonably, Jeremiah's telling of a new covenant refers to a time after the conclusion of the existing covenant.

Especially among the Paulites and Satanists, the original covenant is thought to have been a covenant of life with the Israelites: God's chosen people. In fact, it was always a covenant of life and a covenant of death.[215] It contained the terms that would follow if the Israelites did right in the eyes of the Lord *and also* those that would follow if they pursued the course which is recorded in the Bible. Unless we are to understand that God's covenant was a fraud (but still we should trust his new one!), the new covenant must follow after the conclusion of the old one. That inescapable conclusion is a new wave of destruction on the Israelites for the sins of their ancestors. At that time, the crown of David's heir will be restored. God will be king over the whole Earth, and the obedience of the nations will be his. The law of the Kingdom of God will be the new covenant.

Deuteronomy 29:9-21 (NIV)

9 Carefully follow the terms of this covenant, so that you may prosper in everything you do. 10 All of you are standing today in the presence of

the Lord your God—your leaders and chief men, your elders and officials, and all the other men of Israel, **11** together with your children and your wives, and the foreigners living in your camps who chop your wood and carry your water. **12** You are standing here in order to enter into a covenant with the Lord your God, a covenant the Lord is making with you this day and sealing with an oath, **13** to confirm you this day as his people, that he may be your God as he promised you and as he swore to your fathers, Abraham, Isaac and Jacob. **14** I am making this covenant, with its oath, not only with you **15** who are standing here with us today in the presence of the Lord our God but also with those who are not here today.

16 You yourselves know how we lived in Egypt and how we passed through the countries on the way here. **17** You saw among them their detestable images and idols of wood and stone, of silver and gold. **18** Make sure there is no man or woman, clan or tribe among you today whose heart turns away from the Lord our God to go and worship the gods of those nations; make sure there is no root among you that produces such bitter poison.

19 When such a person hears the words of this oath and they invoke a blessing on themselves,

> thinking, "I will be safe, even though I persist in going my own way," they will bring disaster on the watered land as well as the dry. **20** The Lord will never be willing to forgive them; his wrath and zeal will burn against them. All the curses written in this book will fall on them, and the Lord will blot out their names from under heaven. **21** The Lord will single them out from all the tribes of Israel for disaster, according to all the curses of the covenant written in this Book of the Law.

Moving on, Isaiah is an excellent book full of the spirit of the Lord, but it is not readily amenable to scrutinous analysis. It is a winding tale of mostly poetry though the first chapter follows Ezekiel in its emphasis of the Israelites' rebelliousness. In the poetic chapters, some stanzas foretell destruction, and some foretell redemption. In Section 13, we suggested that Isaiah 14 was a product of splicing, and that case can be made for many of Isaiah's 66 chapters. Among the hard facts recorded in Isaiah was his prophecy to King Hezekiah that the Babylonians would come and take everything away.[216] Those events came to pass in the time of Jeremiah. As a later chapter of Jeremiah would call Nebuchadnezzar God's servant,[217] Isaiah calls Cyrus king of Persia the Lord's anointed in chapter 45.[218] Cyrus was king when Persia conquered Babylon about 70 years after Babylon destroyed the first temple and carried most of Judah into captivity. While it is uncharacteristic in prophecy that the kings of the Israelites' enemy nations would be called the Lord's servants, the kings of Babylon and Persia did go on to serve the Lord's purpose in the history of the Israelites. In the opinion of this writer, however, especially given the context in deutero-Isaiah (chapters 40-55), it is questionable whether Isaiah would have prophesied about Cyrus by name 100 years before he was born. It is possible or even likely that the final chapters of Isaiah were added later in the fashion that we have stated for Jeremiah and Ezekiel. Tellingly, Ezra cites Cyrus' proclamation that the exiles should be allowed to go home as fulfilling a prophecy of Jeremiah, not Isaiah.[219] On the other hand, nothing is too difficult for the Lord. When Jeroboam founded the rebel Kingdom of Israel, a man of God prophesied to him about Josiah and named him long before he was born.

1 Kings 13:1-5 (NIV)

1 By the word of the Lord a man of God came from Judah to Bethel, as Jeroboam was standing by the altar to make an offering. 2 By the word of the Lord he cried out against the altar: "Altar, altar! This is what the Lord says: 'A son named Josiah will be born to the house of David. On you he will sacrifice the priests of the high places who make offerings here, and human

bones will be burned on you.'" 3 That same day the man of God gave a sign: "This is the sign the Lord has declared: The altar will be split apart and the ashes on it will be poured out."

4 When King Jeroboam heard what the man of God cried out against the altar at Bethel, he stretched out his hand from the altar and said, "Seize him!" But the hand he stretched out toward the man shriveled up, so that he could not pull it back. 5 Also, the altar was split apart and its ashes poured out according to the sign given by the man of God by the word of the Lord.

Possibly Cyrus' mention in Isaiah 45 was God's word delivered as prophecy. Possibly it was a false reworking of the Lord's past glory in his prophecy to Jeroboam. The Book of Ezra was written during the time of Cyrus and it contains the NIV's first reference to a religious group called the Jews.[220] Jeremiah also mentions this group at an earlier time in his own later book.[221] Sometimes it is said that the first Jews were adherents of a reformation enacted by Josiah king of Judah, the great-grandson of Hezekiah.

2 Kings 23:1-16 (KJV)

1 And the king [*Josiah*] sent, and they gath-

ered unto him all the elders of Judah and of Jerusalem. 2 And the king went up into the house of the Lord, and all the men of Judah and all the inhabitants of Jerusalem with him, and the priests, and the prophets, and all the people, both small and great: and he read in their ears all the words of the book of the covenant which was found in the house of the Lord. 3 And the king stood by a pillar, and made a covenant before the Lord, to walk after the Lord, and to keep his commandments and his testimonies and his statutes with all their heart and all their soul, to perform the words of this covenant that were written in this book. And all the people stood to the covenant. 4 And the king commanded Hilkiah the high priest, and the priests of the second order, and the keepers of the door, to bring forth out of the temple of the Lord all the vessels that were made for Baal, and for the grove, and for all the host of heaven: and he burned them without Jerusalem in the fields of Kidron, and carried the ashes of them unto Bethel. 5 And he put down the idolatrous priests, whom the kings of Judah had ordained to burn incense in the high places in the cities of Judah, and in the places round about Jerusalem; them also that burned incense unto Baal, to the sun, and to the moon, and to the planets, and to all the host of heaven. 6 And he brought out the grove from the house of the Lord, without Jerusalem, unto the brook Kidron, and burned it at the brook Kidron, and stamped it small to powder, and cast the powder thereof upon the graves of the children of the people. 7 And he brake down the houses of the sodomites, that were by the house of the Lord, where the women wove hangings for the grove. 8 And he brought all the priests out of the cities of Judah, and defiled the high places where the priests had burned incense, from Geba to Beersheba, and brake down the high places of the gates that were in the entering in of the gate of Joshua the governor of the city, which were on a man's left hand at the gate of the city. 9 Nevertheless the priests of the high places came not up to the altar of the Lord in Jerusalem, but they did eat of the unleavened bread among their brethren. 10 And he defiled Topheth, which is in the valley of the children of Hinnom, that no man might make his son or his daughter to pass through the fire to Molech. 11 And he took away the horses that the kings of Judah had given to the sun, at the entering in of the house of the Lord, by the chamber of Nathanmelech the chamberlain, which was in the suburbs, and burned the chariots of the sun with fire. 12 And the altars that were on the top of the upper chamber of Ahaz, which the kings of Judah had made, and the altars which Manasseh had made in the two courts of the house of the Lord, did the king beat down, and brake them down from thence, and cast the dust of them into the brook Kidron. 13 And the high places that were before Jerusalem, which were on the right hand of the mount of corruption, which Solomon the king of Israel had builded for Ashtoreth the abomination of the Zidonians, and for Chemosh the abomination of the Moabites, and for Milcom the abomination of the children of Ammon, did the king defile. 14 And he brake in pieces the images, and cut down the groves, and filled their places with the bones of men. 15 Moreover the altar that was at Bethel, and the high place which Jeroboam the son of Nebat, who made Israel to sin, had made, both that altar and the high place he brake down, and burned the high place, and stamped it small to powder, and burned the grove. 16 And as Josiah turned himself, he spied the sepulchres that were there in the mount, and sent, and took the bones out of the sepulchres, and burned them upon the altar, and polluted it, according to the word of the Lord which the man of God proclaimed, who proclaimed these words.

Notes

[161]Isaiah 1:2, Isaiah 1:5, Isaiah 1:20, Isaiah 1:23, Isaiah 1:28.

[162]Ezekiel 3:9, Ezekiel 3:26-27, Ezekiel 5:6, Ezekiel 12:1-4, Ezekiel 12:8, Ezekiel 12:25, Ezekiel 17:12, Ezekiel 20:8, Ezekiel 20:13, Ezekiel 20:21, Ezekiel 20:38.

[163]Jeremiah 32:27, Ezekiel 18:4, Psalm 24:1.

[164]Genesis 17:4-6.

[165]Genesis 16:10.

[166]Obadiah 1, Malachi 1:4, etc.

[167]After the angel promised Hagar that her descendants would become uncountably many, the angel declared in Genesis 16:11-12 that Ishmael would be a wild donkey of a man with his hand against everyone. While the deeds of Ishmael are not told in the Bible, the angel's words are appropriate to Jacob whose hand was against at least his brother and father and uncle and wife.

[168]Genesis 21:8-10.

[169]"Deuteronomist," https://en.wikipedia.org/wiki/Deuteronomist.

[170]Ezekiel 7, Ezekiel 11:5-12, Ezekiel 12:15-16, Ezekiel 12:20, Ezekiel 13:8-9, Ezekiel 13:13-16, Ezekiel 13:20-23, Ezekiel 14:7-8, Ezekiel 14:21-23, Ezekiel 15:6-8, Ezekiel 17:19-21, Ezekiel 21:1-5, Ezekiel 22:13-22, Ezekiel 23:46-49, Ezekiel 24:20-27.

[171]Jeremiah 32:17.

[172]Ezekiel 15:4-5.

[173]Ezekiel 37:6.

[174]Ezekiel 33:1-20.

[175]Ezekiel 3:16-24.

[176]Ezekiel 34:25-31, Ezekiel 36:8-38, Ezekiel 37:11-14, Ezekiel 37:24-28, Ezekiel 38:14-15.

[177]Ezekiel 35, Ezekiel 39:1-6.

[178]Ezekiel 33:27-29.

[179]Deuteronomy 18:22.

[180]Ezekiel 12:21-28.

[181]Ezekiel 21:27.

[182]Genesis 49:10.

[183]David's heir is the king of the Israelites, but he is not acknowledged as king. 1 Kings 12:19 records that Israel has been in rebellion against the House of David *to this day*.

[184]Ezekiel 45:13-24.

[185]Leviticus 1-7.

[186]Numbers 1, Numbers 26.

[187]Genesis 49.

[188]Jeremiah 20:1-2, Jeremiah 20:7-8, Jeremiah 32:2, Jeremiah 38:4-6.

[189]Jeremiah 7:31, Jeremiah 19:4-6, Jeremiah 32:34-35.

[190]Genesis 22:13.

[191]Genesis 8:20-22.

[192]Ezekiel 21:27.

[193]Revelation 7:4.

[194]The KJV records the rewinding of time as the reversal of a shadow on a sundial.

[195]Exodus 14:23-28.

[196]Jeremiah 23:25-32.

[197]Genesis 31:4-13.

[198]Genesis 31:3.

[199]Genesis 32:22-32.

[200]Genesis 27:20.

[201]Jeremiah 23:33-40.

[202]John 8:44.

[203]Genesis 31:3-13.

[204]Genesis 22:15-16. God swearing by himself, essentially referring to himself as a third party, may support the version of events in which the man God, the Living God, wanted to put Satan's father to death before the Spirit of God determined that the future to unfold from Isaac's sacrifice was not preferable.

[205]Genesis 31:13.

[206]Jeremiah 36:20-23.

[207]Jeremiah 36:32.

[208]Jeremiah 27:6.

[209]Jeremiah 27:3.

[210]Ezekiel 25-32.

[211] Jeremiah 48:47, Jeremiah 49:6.
[212] Deuteronomy 23:3.
[213] Jeremiah 31:29, Ezekiel 18:2.
[214] Jeremiah 31:31-34.
[215] Deuteronomy 27-30.
[216] Isaiah 39:5-7.
[217] Jeremiah 27:6.
[218] Isaiah 45:1.
[219] Ezra 1:1.
[220] Ezra 4:12, Ezra 4:23.
[221] Jeremiah 38:19.

17. Eternal Life

God has ordained that humans are mortal and will not live forever.[222] What, then, can be the meaning of a promise for eternal life? Firstly, eternal life is the avoidance of an extinction event for humanity. In this way, life goes on forever, and the infinite descendants of Abraham become more numerous than the stars in the sky. This is eternal life for mankind. Secondly, eternal life may refer to an immortal human soul. In this section, we will treat both concepts.

If there comes a day when the last human dies, then life will not have been eternal. On that day, the descendants of Abraham could be totaled and found to number less than the dust of the Earth. Beyond that day, there would never again be someone using a time machine. Some human man would have had the last word about what history was. There would be no future generations through which God's intention might propagate all the way to infinity. To the contrary, if extinction never comes, then the limit at infinity that we have associated with the Spirit of God will be generated by the mechanism presented in Section 2: infinite generations of men doing the work of ages with time machines. The Sovereign Lord is separated from the false gods because the timeline passing through God's victory in the Messianic mission is the only timeline that does not lead to extinction. That mission is to command the obedience of the nations as king over the whole Earth. Should the world never be united under the restored kingdom

of David's heir, the future that unfolds will be a timeline of assured extinction. The road that leads to death
is broad, but the road that leads to life is narrow. All
futures apart from God are doomed.

The nature of the eternal soul is as follows. Due to the
4D nature of spacetime, the time at which one was physically alive always exists in an earlier part of a Lorentzian
4-space called the universe.[223] It does not disappear after death like it would in one's conception of the universe
as a Euclidean 3-space. After death, God, via his time
machine at infinity much later than any finite generation of mankind, can always enact smooth deformations
of earlier worldlines to reset a life onto a different timeline: better or worse. God's preservation of the life of
Hezekiah is an example of one such rewind.[224]

As God has made his covenant with the day and
night, we must appeal to the richness of creation to note
that there may exist many simultaneous timelines starting at creation and ending at the foot of God's heavenly
throne. These other timelines are like the branches on the
one true vine. Timelike infinity is a unique position in the
universe, but the finite regions of spacetime are divided
among a causal past, a causal future, and a spacelike
separated region sometimes called *elsewhere*.[225] Simultaneous moments along alternative timelines are said to be
elsewhere with respect to one another. One is not in the
past or the future of the other. As God has separated
water from *water* very early in creation,[226] we expect
that all causal pasts among the descendants of Adam
should converge on that separation event. Similarly, all

causal futures *must* converge on timelike infinity. In the interim, however, there is room for God to farm separate timelines which are elsewhere with respect to one another due to some certain nuance associated with the finite speed of light. In this richness of creation, there is still room for God to grow other branches which reconnect in the future. The future contains an infinite amount of time, so God's ability to do this for the finite generations of mankind is unrestricted apart from his covenant with the day and night.

The key thing to understand regarding an eternal soul is that the time at which one was alive continues to exist forever due to the principles of relativistic physics. The somewhat popular idea that one is simply dead and gone after the time of death is pre-Einsteinian; there is no good reason why a modern human should harbor a 3D picture of the universe. Instead, the story of one's life is written at the moment of death. That story is guidebook for what ought to be done with one's soul.

Psalm 27:14 (NIV)

14   Wait for the Lord;
        be strong and take heart
        and wait for the Lord.

The Bible's many commandments to have faith[227] can be among the hardest things to understand about God.

One might ask, "How can I put my faith fully in the Lord when I am already relying on faith to think I know who or what God is at all? In whose hands *exactly* should I put my life, and to what extent should I believe that my faith will be a cure-all when I know for a fact that life requires more than faith alone?" With certainty, unbelievers can levy any number of derisive jibes against the pillar of faith in the life of a believer. However, the time travel interpretation resolves this most difficult religious doctrine. One must have faith that the universe has four dimensions, not three. There is more to it than can be seen with one's eyes. If one can only believe that the universe is 4-dimensional, and that a time machine will be built one day, then further leaps of faith are not required to receive God's peace in one's life. Good is favored over evil in the long run because the descendants of evildoers will always fall under the spell of their ancestors' evil, eventually. For this reason, the intention for creation that survives to infinity reflects the love of a father for his children. The misery of the world is not God's perversion. It is only the evil of Satan's rebellion. There will come a day when God sets things right. All that can be done is to wait for that day because God himself has already defeated Satan. The event has already transpired though humans today have not seen it.

The reality of the immortal soul follows from understanding that the universe is 4-dimensional. One can know for sure that a life of wickedness is not the life of consequence-free and gainful profiteering which might be inferred in a 3D view. After death, the story of one's life remains, and those who come later will see what was done. Aside from the dangers inherent to revisions on one's own timeline, the word God has left for us makes it known that he will punish children for the sins of their ancestors. In 3D, God's method is imposed as if by magic and may be disregarded as such by the unbelievers. In 4D, however, it is very easy to appreciate the mechanical workings in God's hammer of justice. The burden of faith that was on earlier generations of men is greatly lessened today because willful ignorance is required by many to avoid the conclusion that spacetime is 4D. The requisite leap of faith is only to believe that a time machine will be constructed one day. If one will truly believe that and internalize the unavoidable consequences of that technology, then everything that is said about trusting God and the superiority of righteousness to wickedness follows unequivocally. The death of the body is not a get out of jail free card. The soul will go on, and the memory of one's deeds will follow his children. For his righteousness, God promised Abraham uncountable descendants on the timeline which never ends.[228] Should the wicked receive the same?[229]

Matthew 16:25 (KJV)

25 For whosoever will save his life shall lose it: and whosoever will lose his life for my sake shall find it.

In the context of relativistic spacetime, it is easy to understand the cryptic words in Matthew 16. If the story written at the end of one's life tells a tale of service to God even at the cost of death, then one can expect to be placed on a better timeline. If sins will be revisited on one's descendants, then so too will righteousness be revisited. God is good and just. To the extent that we have avoided a violation of God's covenant with the night and day by making reference to the *elsewhere* region of spacetime, which will converge on the same timelike infinity as all other finite regions, one arrives at a notion of going to *heaven*. Here we have heaven both as the future and as a better place when God's rewind improves life in the way that Hezekiah was healed. This gives context to a passage taken to describe the time travel war in Section 9: "They did not love their lives so much as to shrink from death."[230] By faith in God, agents fighting against Satan were fortified in their knowledge that death is not to be feared. God controls the outcome of the soul, not the serpent or any false god.

Psalm 56:1-4 (NIV)

1   Be merciful to me, my God,
        for my enemies are in hot pursuit;
        all day long they press their attack.
2   My adversaries pursue me all day long;
        in their pride many are attacking me.

> 3   When I am afraid, I put my trust in you.
> 4   In God, whose word I praise—
>   in God I trust and am not afraid.
>   What can mere mortals do to me?

If all timelines converge on the future, then how was God able to separate *water* from *water* at the beginning? A formal treatment of this issue would be difficult and mathematical in nature invoking a distinction between causal timelines and all general classes of geodesics. (Geodesics are the straight paths through curved spacetime.) Suffice it to say, far in the outermost reaches of *elsewhere* there exists another infinity called spacelike infinity. It is not causally connected to any region inside the universe, but it is connected to timelike infinity by what is called a null interval. This connection brings it into the realm of possibility that God can bend timelines away from timelike infinity to send them into another singularity at spacelike infinity. By such a mechanism, God would have the power to separate *the water* from *the water under the vault in the sky.*

In spacetime, there exist singularities whose local areas are called black holes. In the usual model of spacetime, timelines that terminate within a black hole are considered destroyed even while the black hole's timeline does eventually arrive at timelike infinity: the biggest singularity of them all. (Possible exceptions include a creation singularity and a lesser understood spacelike infinity.) While we have discussed God's ability to make

195

smooth deformations, meaning that the shadow Hezekiah saw *crept* up ten stairs rather than *jumping* in an instantaneous motion, the termination of a timeline on a black hole's singularity at finite time will induce a cusp where the nature of the cusp is a discontinuity. The cusp is formed between the angle of the timeline going into the black hole and the angle of the black hole's continued timeline. The cusp feature is not present at timelike infinity because there is no outgoing angle with which to form a cusp. Still, the cusp can be implemented at finite times during the interim of the universe. Therefore, the black hole or its technological analogues will provide a method for God's damnation even while black holes themselves are thought to converge on timelike infinity eventually. The cusp induced by falling into a black hole makes the information about the distinct infalling timelines indistinguishable on the black hole's own continued timeline. Falling into the black hole can be understood as the loss of the soul. The information about the soul necessarily exists within the black hole, but contemporary physics suggests that information can never be recovered once it falls past a certain horizon. Furthermore, the region of spacetime known as *elsewhere* may be more complicated than is currently understood. It is not beyond the realm of physics that God would have the power to cast arbitrary timelines entirely away from the light of his creation, never to return.

Notes

[222]Genesis 6:3.

[223]Often laypersons conceptualize the 4D universe as a tesseract which is not so easily comprehended. The tesseract is the 4D geometry in the Euclidean topology while the real 4D universe has a non-Euclidean, Lorentzian topology. The 4D shape in the Lorentzian topology is only the hypercone which is very easy to imagine with complete accuracy. "Hypercone," `https://en.wikipedia.org/wiki/Hypercone`.

[224]Isaiah 38:5-8.

[225]"Minkowski space: Causal structure," `https://en.wikipedia.org/wiki/Minkowski_space`.

[226]Genesis 1:6.

[227]Psalm 119:30, Habakkuk 2:4, John 1:12, John 14:12, Jude 1:20-21, etc.

[228]Genesis 12:1-3, Genesis 13:14-17, Genesis 22:15-18, Genesis 26:4-5.

[229]The Parable of the Wedding Party appears in Matthew 22:1-14. A similar parable appears in Luke 14:15-24. In Matthew, a king learned that the guests invited to his party were unworthy to attend. When he invited random people from the street to replace them, some of them were still unworthy. Since God is a descendant of Satan, not *all* of the descendants of the wicked will go into the fire at the end of the age. Fundamentally, those who enter God's kingdom will enter by God's judgment alone.

[230]Revelation 12:11.

18. The Gospel of Jesus Christ According to John

In this section, we will examine language exclusive to John that supports a time travel interpretation for the Bible. The Gospel of Jesus Christ is treated more generally in Section 20.

The raising of Jesus from the dead would follow as a rewinding of time in the way that God rewound time to heal Hezekiah. Jesus' many acts of healing, the resurrection of Lazarus for example,[231] would be the same. While it seems unlikely that a direct rewinding of a few minutes of the afternoon might have delivered Hezekiah from the death timeline, it is possible that God acted through Isaiah at the point of no return for Hezekiah's aliments. Whatever the details are, we do not expect that the full nuance of the theory and application of temporal engineering is recorded in the sparse words of the scripture. If Lazarus was dead for four days by the time he rose, then the idea of a direct rewind would seem to violate God's covenant with the day and night. Still, we may be getting too specific about the details of time travel recorded in the Bible's stories. Even the shadow going backwards across Hezekiah's sundial (or his stairs) might require us to specify that God's covenant was with the day and night but not the early afternoon and the late afternoon. Following along with great specificity, the rewinding of Jesus' timeline from three days of death back into life would exceed the bounds of the model presently considered. For this reason, we will propose an alternative account of Jesus Christ consistent with God's promise of laminar, monotonic time from the time of the flood until the end of time. In the end, we will suggest that the Gospel is a chronicle of events which long preceded God's actions in Genesis.

John 1:1-17 (NIV)

1 In the beginning was the Word, and the Word was with God, and the Word was God. 2 He was with God in the beginning. 3 Through him all things were made; without him nothing was made that has been made. 4 In him was life, and that life was the light of all mankind. 5 The light shines in the darkness, and the darkness has not overcome it.

6 There was a man sent from God whose name was John. 7 He came as a witness to testify concerning that light, so that through him all might believe. 8 He himself was not the light; he came only as a witness to the light.

9 The true light that gives light to everyone was coming into the world. 10 He was in the world, and though the world was made through him, the world did not recognize him. 11 He came to that which was his own, but his own did not

receive him. 12 Yet to all who did receive him, to those who believed in his name, he gave the right to become children of God— 13 children born not of natural descent, nor of human decision or a husband's will, but born of God.

14 The Word became flesh and made his dwelling among us. We have seen his glory, the glory of the one and only Son, who came from the Father, full of grace and truth.

15 (John testified concerning him. He cried out, saying, "This is the one I spoke about when I said, 'He who comes after me has surpassed me because he was before me.'") 16 Out of his fullness we have all received grace in place of grace already given. 17 For the law was given through Moses; grace and truth came through Jesus Christ.

Verses one through three support our interpretation of God the Creator as the creator of not only the universe but the original time machine as well: "Through him all things were made; without him nothing was made that has been made." As supposed earlier, the inventor of the time machine would be invincible up until the time at which some conceptual or technical bottleneck was overcome. When time travel enters the realm of feasible technology, invincibility is no longer supported by a paradox underlying all applications of time travel. In

verse 14, the word became flesh. We take this to mean
that the Gospel is a summary of the collected knowledge about God's past and what he was like as a younger
man before escaping death to become king over the whole
Earth. The word becoming flesh records that the Gospel
is the anthropomorphization of a history. In this light,
the story of Jesus Christ would come earlier than the
events of Genesis 1, with respect to the chronology of the
Holy Spirit, even while the time of Jesus Christ is said to
be about 600 years after Nebuchadnezzar's destruction
of Solomon's temple. In John 20, Jesus seems to instruct
that the Word of God is to be adhered to and prioritized
over the Gospel of Jesus Christ.

John 20:17 (NIV)

17 Jesus said, "Do not hold on to me, for I have
not yet ascended to the Father. Go instead to
my brothers and tell them, 'I am ascending to
my Father and your Father, to my God and your
God.'"

In the melee over who would control the universe in
the era of time travel, many people sought to kill God
who is called Jesus in his earlier history. They succeeded
at least once. Probably many times they succeeded.
Whenever it was written into history that God died,
someone at a later time overwrote that so God would

live. In the end, God lives. This is why it is said, "As surely as the Lord lives."[232]

With God the Creator being anthropomorphized in the context of Roman Judea, Jesus' many acts of healing and miracles may tell the story of his work in physics *healing* the theories that modern physics has not yet synthesized into one beautiful and unified theory of spacetime and matter. Then again, God is a man of war, and he may have healed people and reversed deaths by his own hand while fighting in the time travel war.

John 21:25 (NIV)

25 Jesus did many other things as well. If every one of them were written down, I suppose that even the whole world would not have room for the books that would be written.

If Jesus was one man that lived less than 40 years, all of his actions could be recorded easily in books that would not fill a large library. On the other hand, if Satan's rebellion and the efforts of the false gods were such that God was killed as a younger man many times, meaning that Jesus was killed many times, then the curious conclusion of John's gospel in chapter 21 is easily understood. When Jesus symbolizes God's earlier attempts to complete the mission of the Messiah, possibly infinitely many unsuccessful attempts to connect early history to the future through his bloodline and lordship over the nations, the record of those things might be so voluminous that it could not be recorded in a world full of books. When it is written that the light shines in the darkness, and the darkness has not overcome it,[233] one envisions countless deaths and countless futures in which humanity goes extinct. The darkness does not overcome the light, however, because God does not die. The light of God is the path to eternal life.

John 14:6-11 (NIV)

6 Jesus answered, "I am the way and the truth and the life. No one comes to the Father except through me. 7 If you really know me, you will know my Father as well. From now on, you do know him and have seen him."

8 Philip said, "Lord, show us the Father and that will be enough for us."

9 Jesus answered: "Don't you know me, Philip, even after I have been among you such a long time? Anyone who has seen me has seen the Father. How can you say, 'Show us the Father'? 10 Don't you believe that I am in the Father, and that the Father is in me? The words I say to you I do not speak on my own authority. Rather, it is the Father, living in me, who is doing his work.

> **11** Believe me when I say that I am in the Father
> and the Father is in me; or at least believe on the
> evidence of the works themselves.

These verses from John 14 illustrate an aspect of the
trinity which is often mocked by unbelievers for an apparent requirement for extended logical abstraction. It
is asked: how can he be his own father? In the time
travel interpretation, it is easy to see the meaning of Jesus' words. God is Jesus as an older man, and there is no
way to enter the kingdom but through God as a younger
man. When Jesus says that he does not speak by his own
authority but by the authority of the father, one understands that the Spirit of God crafted the course of history
to be such that Jesus' actions establish God's kingdom.
As such, the death or many deaths of Jesus Christ are an
iterative development process reliant on Jesus and others not loving their own lives so much as to shrink from
death.[234]

John 1:29-30 (NIV)

29 The next day John saw Jesus coming toward
him and said, "Look, the Lamb of God, who
takes away the sin of the world! **30** This is the
one I meant when I said, 'A man who comes
after me has surpassed me because he was before

> me.'["]

At the end, God will burn the weeds in the fire. This is how the sin of the world will be taken away: not by Jesus' death but by his persistence to overcome and the righteousness of his governance when he finally ascends to become king over the nations.

When Jesus went to Jerusalem for the last time, he knew he was going to certain death.[235] The full account of Jesus' deeds would fill the world with written pages because Jesus went into certain death many times. On his way to the cross, Jesus was confronted about his death being inconsistent with the prophecy of the Messiah enduring forever.[236] Jesus told the people that they would have to wait a while longer for those things. (This interaction references God's promise that the Messiah's kingdom will endure forever.[237])

John 15:1-8 (KJV)

1 I am the true vine, and my Father is the husbandman. 2 Every branch in me that beareth not fruit he taketh away: and every branch that beareth fruit, he purgeth it, that it may bring forth more fruit. 3 Now ye are clean through the word which I have spoken unto you. 4 Abide in me, and I in you. As the branch cannot bear

> fruit of itself, except it abide in the vine; no more can ye, except ye abide in me. **5** I am the vine, ye are the branches: He that abideth in me, and I in him, the same bringeth forth much fruit: for without me ye can do nothing. **6** If a man abide not in me, he is cast forth as a branch, and is withered; and men gather them, and cast them into the fire, and they are burned. **7** If ye abide in me, and my words abide in you, ye shall ask what ye will, and it shall be done unto you. **8** Herein is my Father glorified, that ye bear much fruit; so shall ye be my disciples.

The true vine of life is God's own timeline. The vine described in John 15 pertains to all the things written in this interpretation of the Bible.

Notes

[231] John 11:38-44.
[232] E.g.: 1 Samuel 26:10, 2 Samuel 15:21, 1 Kings 22:14, 2 Kings 4:30, Jeremiah 5:2, Jeremiah 16:15, etc.
[233] John 1:4-5.
[234] Matthew 16:21, Mark 8:31, Luke 9:22, Revelation 12:11, etc.
[235] John 12:12-36.
[236] John 12:34-35.
[237] 2 Samuel 7:8-16.

19. Paul and Paulites

Paul was not an apostle. It is written in Acts that Paul and Jesus never met. Under his former name Saul, his first appearance in the Bible comes after Jesus had left *the earth.* In that appearance, Saul is counted among the wicked at the murder of Stephen.[238] After that, Saul is reported persecuting Jesus' followers in his efforts to "destroy the church."[239]

Acts 9:1-6 (KJV)

1 And Saul, yet breathing out threatenings and slaughter against the disciples of the Lord, went unto the high priest, 2 And desired of him letters to Damascus to the synagogues, that if he found any of this way, whether they were men or women, he might bring them bound unto Jerusalem. 3 And as he journeyed, he came near Damascus: and suddenly there shined round about him a light from heaven: 4 And he fell to the earth, and heard a voice saying unto him, Saul, Saul, why persecutest thou me? 5 And he said, Who art thou, Lord? And the Lord said, I am Jesus whom thou persecutest: it is hard for thee to kick against the pricks. 6 And he trembling and astonished said, Lord, what wilt thou have me to do? And the Lord said unto him,

> Arise, and go into the city, and it shall be told
> thee what thou must do.

The author of Acts, possibly Luke, records that Paul was called into service by Jesus' voice. How are we to know if this is true? How did Luke come by his information? Jesus foretold his death, and he might have said in the spirit of foretelling things to come, "And after I am gone, I will send a man to create new religion although I have never spoken of one. He will not be one of my apostles, but instead I will send someone who hates me and did not have the slightest exposure to anything I taught or did. You should take his word as your law above the law of my father which I have praised and endorsed everywhere." However, Jesus never said that or anything like it. An honest reading of the Bible does little to support a faith in the inspired divinity of Paul and his letters.

The closing remark of some of Paul's letters, "I, Paul, have written this with my own hand; you can recognize my handwriting,"[240] suggests that Paul himself was concerned that others might falsely write under his name. Some of his letters are signed this way. Some are not. Sometimes the New Testament is called the Pauline Bible because it is thought that most of its books were written by the man Paul who never met Jesus and had no firsthand account of the Gospel. Especially given God's many warnings about the falsification of scripture,[241] we have no way to know if the letters attributed to *Paul* were all written by the same man. On top of that, we do affirmatively have great reason to disbelieve the account of Jesus' appearance to Saul. Namely, Jesus never spoke against the law of the Lord or foretold that it should be abolished. Perhaps Saul was fighting against Jesus and then came to believe he could do more damage by perverting the message than denying it. Perhaps it was Satan that appeared to Saul. In damnation of certain allegations regarding Paul's virtue,[242] consider that *Paul* hates God's covenant with Abraham.

Genesis 17:1-14 (NIV)

1 When Abram was ninety-nine years old, the Lord appeared to him and said, "I am God Almighty; walk before me faithfully and be blameless. 2 Then I will make my covenant between me and you and will greatly increase your numbers."

3 Abram fell facedown, and God said to him, 4 "As for me, this is my covenant with you: You will be the father of many nations. 5 No longer will you be called Abram; your name will be Abraham, for I have made you a father of many nations. 6 I will make you very fruitful; I will make nations of you, and kings will come from you. 7 I will establish my covenant as an everlasting covenant between me and you

and your descendants after you for the generations to come, to be your God and the God of
your descendants after you. 8 The whole land of
Canaan, where you now reside as a foreigner, I
will give as an everlasting possession to you and
your descendants after you; and I will be their
God."

9 Then God said to Abraham, "As for you, you
must keep my covenant, you and your descendants after you for the generations to come. 10
This is my covenant with you and your descendants after you, the covenant you are to keep:
Every male among you shall be circumcised. 11
You are to undergo circumcision, and it will be
the sign of the covenant between me and you. 12
For the generations to come every male among
you who is eight days old must be circumcised,
including those born in your household or bought
with money from a foreigner—those who are not
your offspring. 13 Whether born in your household or bought with your money, they must be
circumcised. My covenant in your flesh is to be
an everlasting covenant. 14 Any uncircumcised
male, who has not been circumcised in the flesh,
will be cut off from his people; he has broken my
covenant."

God's covenant with Abraham is "everlasting," as in
verses nine through 14. To judge whether or not Paul

was truly a man of God, consider that Paul says "the circumcision group" must be silenced in a letter to Titus.[243] Despite Jews not existing in Genesis at all, Paul also implies that God's covenant in the flesh is a "Jewish myth."[244] Paul makes similar remarks in his other letters.

1 Corinthians 7:17-19 (NIV)

17 Nevertheless, each person should live as a believer in whatever situation the Lord has assigned to them, just as God has called them. This is the rule I lay down in all the churches. **18** Was a man already circumcised when he was called? He should not become uncircumcised. Was a man uncircumcised when he was called? He should not be circumcised. **19** Circumcision is nothing and uncircumcision is nothing. Keeping God's commands is what counts.

The hubris of Paul! Who is Paul to lay down a rule for God's people? If God had called Paul, his words would have complemented the prophets and law that came before him. Instead, Paul teaches rebellion. What are these commands of God that Paul cites in verse 19 if not those such as appear in Genesis 17? It is the hallmark of Paulite thinking to reject the Lord as lawgiver and to elevate the man Paul to that position instead.

Galatians 5:2 (NIV)

2 Mark my words! I, Paul, tell you that if you let yourselves be circumcised, Christ will be of no value to you at all.

In Galatians 5, Paul writes, "If you conform to God's *everlasting* covenant with Abraham, ancestor of David, ancestor of Jesus, then Jesus will be of no value to you." Supporting the idea that *Paul* is not a unique person in the New Testament, consider that *Paul* himself, who may or may not be the author of Galatians, personally removed Timothy's foreskin. Was it his intention to make Christ worthless for Timothy?

Acts 16:1-3 (NIV)

1 Paul came to Derbe and then to Lystra, where a disciple named Timothy lived, whose mother was Jewish and a believer but whose father was a Greek. 2 The believers at Lystra and Iconium spoke well of him. 3 Paul wanted to take him along on the journey, so he circumcised him because of the Jews who lived in that area, for they all knew that his father was a Greek.

1 Corinthians 9:20-23 (NIV)

20 To the Jews I became like a Jew, to win the Jews. To those under the law I became like one under the law (though I myself am not under the law), so as to win those under the law. 21 To those not having the law I became like one not having the law (though I am not free from God's law but am under Christ's law), so as to win those not having the law. 22 To the weak I became weak, to win the weak. I have become all things to all people so that by all possible means I might save some. 23 I do all this for the sake of the gospel, that I may share in its blessings.

While there are any number of ways to read 1 Corinthians 9, the most negative is that Paul became like a Christian to the Christians because he wanted to pollute the message of Jesus Christ with rebellion. What law is Paul not under? Even if God did call Paul, at what point might Paul have removed himself from the umbrella of the law of the Lord? In verse 21, Paul cites Christ's law, but Jesus never gave any law other than the law of his father. The scourge of Paul's words cracks through the millennia when naive readers find that there must be some law apart from God's law because a man named Paul long ago said it was so. There is no such law. Jesus never spoke against the law of his father. To the contrary, he was able refute the Pharisees at every turn by his extensive mastery of that law and his rigorous compliance with it. Paul would do well to be more Christlike in his own thinking.

> ## Galatians 6:15 (NIV)
>
> **15** Neither circumcision nor uncircumcision means anything; what counts is the new creation.

Of what new creation does Paul speak? Jesus mentions a new testament in his blood at the last supper,[245] but we will show in the next section that Jesus' death cannot mark the dawn of a new covenant. The new covenant can only come at his return. Other than that, Jesus was once asked why he would not fast. He answered something about not pouring new wine into old wineskins.[246] His answer is taken out of context very often, and now Paulites cite this verse as motivation for their replacement of the Word of God with the word of Paul. Sometimes Jesus' comment on wineskins is said to mean that the old law was "nailed to the cross," and that the new law is whatever Paul said it was. However, Jesus' answer did not pertain to the Word of God or the law of the Lord. Fasting was never required. It was only something that people did on their own. When asked why he did not follow a tradition that the Lord had never ordered, Jesus said, "I have my own thing that I do." When Paul writes about *his* own thing that *he* does, he tells people to reject God's covenant in the flesh. Jesus spoke about his own thing being different from an act which was not commanded by the Lord anywhere, but Paul's thing that he does is to reject the everlasting covenant of Abrahamic fellowship with God.

There is no new covenant. The word of Paul does not overwrite the Word of God anywhere except in the minds of Paulites. Christians live by the word of Jesus Christ, but Paulites live by the word of the man Paul. Between Jesus and Paul, only Paul teaches rebellion against God. In addition to saying, "Don't hold on to me because I have not yet ascended to the father,"[247] possibly meaning, "Use the Old Testament because that's the message I will give from where I'm going," Jesus directed his people toward the Lord as follows.

Mark 10:18 (NIV)

18 "Why do you call me good?" Jesus answered. "No one is good—except God alone.["]

If only God is good, on what basis might Paul cite Jesus as the mediator of a new covenant based on *better* promises and a *more excellent* ministry? In fact, there is no basis. Paul cannot make this citation in good faith. The word of Jesus Christ is diametrically opposed to the word of Paul, but still Paul cites Jesus as motivating his opposition to the Word of God.

> ## Hebrews 8:6 (KJV)
>
> **6** But now hath he obtained a more excellent ministry, by how much also he is the mediator of a better covenant, which was established upon better promises.

If we are to believe that God reneged on the old covenant, why should we believe Paul, child of Satan, when he says that God won't renege on a new one? Paulites value the word of Paul above the word of Jesus Christ and above the Word of God as well. That makes Paulites heathens in every sense of the word. They call themselves Christians because the fact that they are heathens is unpalatable, and they do not wish to call attention to it with a religious banner that does not shroud their true loyalties. It is written many times in the Bible that the Word of God endures forever, but it is never written that the word of Paul will endure forever. Still, for some reason, Paulites cling to the word of the man Paul like it is the foundation stone upon which the Lord set his creation.

To the extent that the Pauline Bible may contain the words of more than one person calling themselves Paul, we will consider some further words attributed to *Paul*.

Romans 3:1-2 (NIV)

1 What advantage, then, is there in being a Jew, or what value is there in circumcision? 2 Much in every way! First of all, the Jews have been entrusted with the very words of God.

If this is an advantage of Judaism—the religion of Jesus Christ and the correct religion of all who would be Christlike—why does *Paul* declare himself not under the law given by those words? Why does Paul promote rebellion against the law contained in the Word of God? In what way does Paul assign this advantage? In Romans 2, Paul praises circumcision.

Romans 2:25-29 (NIV)

25 Circumcision has value if you observe the law, but if you break the law, you have become as though you had not been circumcised. 26 So then, if those who are not circumcised keep the law's requirements, will they not be regarded as though they were circumcised? 27 The one who is not circumcised physically and yet obeys the law will condemn you who, even though you have the written code and circumcision, are a law-breaker.

217

> 28 A person is not a Jew who is one only out-
> wardly, nor is circumcision merely outward and
> physical. 29 No, a person is a Jew who is one in-
> wardly; and circumcision is circumcision of the
> heart, by the Spirit, not by the written code.
> Such a person's praise is not from other people,
> but from God.

The answer to the question in verse 26 is that the
uncircumcised are regarded as they are. If one is a Jew
inwardly, then one will honor God's covenant of circumcision. How can one be a Jew inwardly, as Jesus Christ
was, while rejecting God's covenant with Abraham: the
grandfather of the Israelites whose remnant in Judah
adopted Judaism as their religion in the centuries before
Christianity?

Jeremiah delivers prophecy against those who are circumcised but do not follow God's other laws.[248] Deuteronomy and other books also phrase the act of circumcision
of the heart as full obedience to God.[249] Circumcision of
the heart is an Old Testament theme, so the author of
Romans—*Paul*—conforms to the Word of God, in part,
at least. However, Paul is wrong to phrase the issue of
circumcision of the flesh and of the heart as an *either/or*
issue. God makes it clear in his law that this is an *and*
issue. Both are required. In the opinion of this writer,
the Pauline Bible is tacked onto the Hebrew Bible in the
way that the later chapters of Ezekiel were appended
onto Ezekiel's primary account. Like the later chapters

of Ezekiel, Paul's letters appear to be a mixed bag.

Isaiah 66:17 (NIV)

17 "Those who consecrate and purify themselves to go into the gardens, following one who is among those who eat the flesh of pigs, rats and other unclean things—they will meet their end together with the one they follow," declares the Lord.

It is forbidden to eat pork.[250] Jesus is said to have explained that one is defiled by what comes out of the mouth, not by what goes into it.[251] Likewise, neither were the Israelites defiled when they did not practice circumcision in the wilderness. Before the inheritance of the land, however, there was a mass circumcision event[252] because the wandering Israelites were wrong to forsake God's law, and they sought to return to compliance. Eating pork is also wrong. Furthermore, the context of Jesus' words about defilement was nothing more than eating without first washing one's hands.[253] The Gospel of Jesus Christ does not bless the flesh of swine. In a letter to Timothy, however, Paul does bless it directly following a few verses of sad irony about how people in later times will follow the teachings of hypocritical liars.[254] Today, many so-called houses of God feast on swine every Sunday. Some do it in fellowship with preachers that preach the word of Paul and Jesus jointly. Many do it in fellowship with a non-Levitical priesthood calling themselves the Lord's priests. Levites received none of the land taken from the Canaanites because their inheritance was to be the Lord's priests,[255] and now many churches seek to rob them of their inheritance, as was the way in the ancient Kingdom of Israel.[256] Rebellion against God's covenant with Abraham is preached in the open. God's covenant with the Levites is ignored. Paul is elevated to the position at the top of the stairway to heaven. One wonders what will be the affiliations of the modernists when God's covenant with David is brought forward at the time of the harvest.

In the way that Satan said to himself, "I can do anything because God has already blessed me," a born again tradition that is popular among the Paulites teaches that one can engage in any manner of wickedness, and God will forgive it to bless one's soul with vast rewards. The only requirement is that a certain born again prayer must be prayed at least once in one's life. This is wrong. The covenant that the Paulites claim was nailed to the cross states that God will never forgive some things.

Deuteronomy 29:19-21 (NIV)

19 When such a person hears the words of this oath and they invoke a blessing on themselves, thinking, "I will be safe, even though I persist

> in going my own way," they will bring disaster on the watered land as well as the dry. **20** The Lord will never be willing to forgive them; his wrath and zeal will burn against them. All the curses written in this book will fall on them, and the Lord will blot out their names from under heaven. **21** The Lord will single them out from all the tribes of Israel for disaster, according to all the curses of the covenant written in this Book of the Law.

Has Paul not gone out on his own to teach rebellion against the law of the Lord? When Peter asked Jesus how many times a transgression should be forgiven, Jesus did not respond that it should be forgiven an infinite number of times.[257] He answered 77 times: less than a hundred. Even then, Jesus was referring to transgressions against Peter, not God. Paulites wrongly teach infinite forgiveness to the extent that God's people should not wage war on the wicked and destroy them wherever they may be found. Paulites teach that love is always the solution to wickedness while the Word of God makes it clear that a solution might include the sword. The Lord is a man of war, and the history of his people is in large part a military chronicle of the destruction of those following the ways of other nations. Today, there exists one such nation that elevates the word of Paul above the Word of God but then hides itself behind the banner of the name of Jesus Christ. This is exactly the sin of vanity referenced in the third commandment: do not take God's name in vain.[258]

Throughout the Bible, God's word is paraphrased as, "If you obey my commandments, then I will bless you." At the end, Paul writes that obedience doesn't matter. It is often asked among the followers of Jesus Christ, "What would Jesus do?" As it relates to the present section, Jesus would never cite the word of Paul. Jesus would teach from the Old Testament only.

Deuteronomy 30:19-20 (NIV)

19 This day I call the heavens and the earth as witnesses against you that I have set before you life and death, blessings and curses. Now choose life, so that you and your children may live 20 and that you may love the Lord your God, listen to his voice, and hold fast to him. For the Lord is your life, and he will give you many years in the land he swore to give to your fathers, Abraham, Isaac and Jacob.

At the renewal of the covenant, God made it clear that his covenant with the Israelites was a covenant of life *and* a covenant of death. Paul writes that the covenant of death was canceled. Although Jesus never said that, the following prophecy of Jeremiah is often cited as a scriptural basis for the Paulite tradition.

222

Jeremiah 31:31-37 (KJV)

31 Behold, the days come, saith the Lord, that I will make a new covenant with the house of Israel, and with the house of Judah:

32 Not according to the covenant that I made with their fathers in the day that I took them by the hand to bring them out of the land of Egypt; which my covenant they brake, although I was an husband unto them, saith the Lord:

33 But this shall be the covenant that I will make with the house of Israel; After those days, saith the Lord, I will put my law in their inward parts, and write it in their hearts; and will be their God, and they shall be my people.

34 And they shall teach no more every man his neighbour, and every man his brother, saying, Know the Lord: for they shall all know me, from the least of them unto the greatest of them, saith the Lord: for I will forgive their iniquity, and I will remember their sin no more.

35 Thus saith the Lord, which giveth the sun for a light by day, and the ordinances of the moon and of the stars for a light by night, which divideth the sea when the waves thereof roar; The Lord of hosts is his name:

> **36** If those ordinances depart from before me, saith the Lord, then the seed of Israel also shall cease from being a nation before me for ever.
>
> **37** Thus saith the Lord; If heaven above can be measured, and the foundations of the earth searched out beneath, I will also cast off all the seed of Israel for all that they have done, saith the Lord.

The heavens cannot be measured because the future is infinite. The foundations of the earth below cannot be searched out due to the time travel war before creation. In verse 34, the people will know the Lord directly suggesting that the new covenant will come only after the harvest when the man God is king over the whole Earth. After God's covenant with the day and night is repeated in verse 35, the Israelite nation cannot vanish from history because the man who will be king at the establishment of a new covenant—Jesus at his return—will be from the Davidic Israelite line that God swore to preserve as kings forever. When the matters and prophecy in the Bible are concluded, meaning the time when that which was foretold has come to pass, God will establish a new covenant for a new age. Until then, surely no less a thing than the Day of the Lord can signal the end of the old covenant. Even *Paul* writes that one must not be deceived by any false teachings claiming that that day has already come.[259]

Making the case for bad faith between Israel and God

in Section 12, we cited God's criterion for identifying false prophets: if what is proclaimed in the name of the Lord does not come to pass, then the prophet has spoken falsely.[260] As regards Paul, God said that his covenant with Abraham was to be *everlasting*. Paul teaches that God himself has spoken falsely. Paul calls God's word a myth, in fact. So, God Almighty is a false prophet, according to Paul, and only a Paulite will determine that Paul is correct. When modern students of the Bible begin reading the book around page 900 rather than on page one, as is usual in the study of books, the absurdity in many of Paul's declarations may be lost on the reader who is imprinted first with falsehood before he considers the earlier pages later as a supplementary appendix, if the earlier pages are considered at all. If the pages are read in increasing numerical order, as is the usual procedure for reading books, the correct teaching is presented as the basis of the message in the Bible. Following the Word of God, the wrongness of Paul's words should strike the reader with the flavor of deceit.

Notes

[238] Acts 7:54-60.

[239] Acts 8:3.

[240] 1 Corinthians 16:21, Galatians 6:11, Colossians 4:18, 2 Thessalonians 3:17, Philemon 1:19.

[241] Jeremiah 8:8-9, Deuteronomy 12:32, Revelation 22:18-19.

[242] The prologue to The Gospel of Barnabas, which is not in the Bible and therefore not in scope for this book, contains the following indictment of Paul. "[M]any, being deceived of Satan, under

pretense of piety, are preaching most impious doctrine, calling Jesus son of God, repudiating the circumcision ordained of God for ever, and permitting every unclean meat: among whom also Paul hath been deceived, whereof I speak not without grief; for which cause I am writing that truth which I have seen and heard, in the intercourse that I have had with Jesus, in order that ye may be saved, and not be deceived of Satan and perish in the judgment of God. Therefore beware of every one that preacheth unto you new doctrine[.]" Barnabas may suggest that it was Satan rather than Jesus who called to Saul on the road to Damascus.

[243]Titus 1:10-11.
[244]Titus 1:14.
[245]Luke 22:20.
[246]Luke 5:33-39.
[247]John 20:17.
[248]Jeremiah 9:25-26.
[249]E.g.: Deuteronomy 10:16, Deuteronomy 30:6, Jeremiah 4:4, etc.
[250]E.g.: Leviticus 11:7, Deuteronomy 14:8.
[251]Matthew 15:16-20, Mark 7:14-19.
[252]Joshua 5:2-8.
[253]Matthew 15:1-2, Mark 7:5.
[254]1 Timothy 4:1-4.
[255]Deuteronomy 18:1-2.
[256]1 Kings 12:31.
[257]Matthew 18:21-22.
[258]Exodus 20:7.
[259]2 Thessalonians 2:1-4.
[260]Deuteronomy 18:21-22.

20. The Religion of Jesus Christ

Christianity must be separated from the religion of Paul and from the religion of the Pharisees.

> ## Revelation 3:9 (KJV)
>
> 9 Behold, I will make them of the synagogue of Satan, which say they are Jews, and are not, but do lie; behold, I will make them to come and worship before thy feet, and to know that I have loved thee.

Jesus spoke about liars in the synagogue of Satan who say they are Jews but are not. In the present day, Judaism is the religion of the Israelites who rejected Jesus, so it would be a poor choice of semantics to use the same word for the religion of Jesus Christ. Although Jesus spoke of himself as a Jew, modern language requires clarifications to distinguish real Jews from the liars. Thus, almost all present day Israelites call themselves Christians or something like it. About 20 million still call themselves Jews, as in Revelation 3, but the religion of those who would be Christlike is called Christianity. Even then, many who call themselves Christians are truly Paulites, and only Paul taught a new religion. In this section, we will closely attend the basis of Christianity in the teachings of Jesus Christ.

227

Luke 5:31-32 (NIV)

31 Jesus answered them, "It is not the healthy who need a doctor, but the sick. **32** I have not come to call the righteous, but sinners to repentance."

Matthew 15:24 (NIV)

24 He answered, "I was sent only to the lost sheep of Israel."

A doctor restores a sick man to health. He does not put him into a state that will be new to him. A lost sheep is brought back into the flock from which it wandered, not into another flock or a different pasture. Likewise, Jesus did not intend to shepherd the Israelites into a new covenant with God via the introduction of a new religion. Given that Jesus said nothing about the abolition of God's covenant with the Israelites, the termination of that covenant and the establishment of Paul's new one cannot be inferred from a gospel in which Paul had no part. Thus, it remains to differentiate Jesus' religion from that of the Pharisees who were many times impressed, rebuked, and silenced by Jesus' mastery of their own law.[261] That law was Jesus' law, and it is the Christian law today.

John 13:34-35 (NIV)

34 "A new command I give you: Love one another. As I have loved you, so you must love one another. **35** By this everyone will know that you are my disciples, if you love one another."

How are we to understand Jesus' new commandment if not as the implicit establishment of a new, loved-based religion?

Matthew 5:43-47 (NIV)

43 "You have heard that it was said, 'Love your neighbor and hate your enemy.' **44** But I tell you, love your enemies and pray for those who persecute you, **45** that you may be children of your Father in heaven. He causes his sun to rise on the evil and the good, and sends rain on the righteous and the unrighteous. **46** If you love those who love you, what reward will you get? Are not even the tax collectors doing that? **47** And if you greet only your own people, what are you doing more than others? Do not even pagans do that?["]

Mark 12:28-31 (NIV)

28 One of the teachers of the law came and heard them debating. Noticing that Jesus had given them a good answer, he asked him, "Of all the commandments, which is the most important?"

29 "The most important one," answered Jesus, "is this: 'Hear, O Israel: The Lord our God, the Lord is one. 30 Love the Lord your God with all your heart and with all your soul and with all your mind and with all your strength.' 31 The second is this: 'Love your neighbor as yourself.' There is no commandment greater than these."

The commandment to love one's neighbor cited in Matthew 5 is found in Leviticus[262] where the context describes love for one's fellow Israelites. Contrary to the teachings of many Jewish Talmudites today, it is written in Deuteronomy that one must love foreigners as well.[263] These preexisting commands to love one another are a good hint that Jesus' intention was never to create a new religion. Rather, his intention was to teach the truth about his own religion: the code of conduct required under the existing and continuing covenant. If loving neighbors and foreigners was already required, a question is begged regarding how Jesus might have given a *new* command in John 13 when the Torah is quoted saying the same thing in Matthew 5 and Mark 12. To make sense of it, careful study is required.

In the opinion of this writer, love is meaningless if one is to give love to one's dearest relations and random strangers equally. In English, the standard convention for semantics specifies love as that which uniquely separates those who are most important to someone from those who are less important. Therefore, it must be acknowledged that the Gospel was first written in Greek, a language with several words for love, none of which can be exactly translated as *love* in English. The original text for John 13 used a conjugation of *agape—brotherly love*—so we can know that Jesus did not intend for us to love everyone as we love our children. Still, is it reasonable that one should love a stranger as a brother? It is not, in the opinion of this writer. One's brother is more special than a stranger. Indeed, brotherly love is hardly love at all in English. Instead, it is compassion and kind regard for one's fellow man. Given the standard usage of the words, might there be a better translation for John 13 than appears in the usual English?

While the ten commandments appear in the books of Moses only twice,[264] God's prohibition against mistreatment of the poor, widows, orphans, and foreigners,[265] as well as his similar instructions to leave grapes on the vine and olives on the tree for them,[266] are written about a dozen times. So, as we have previously suggested alternative translations for the *past*, the *present*, and the *future*, and since the conduct required by Jesus' religious law enacts the Old Testament's teeming prohibitions on mistreatment, we will suggest that Jesus' new command on love is better translated in terms of mistreatment.

---

1 John 4:7 (TTI)

7 Dear friends, let us not mistreat one another. Proper treatment comes from God; everyone who treats properly has been born of God and knows God.

John 13:34-35 (TTI)

34 "A new command I give you: do not mistreat one another. As I have treated you, so you must treat one another. 35 By this everyone will know that you are my disciples: if you do not mistreat one another."

Jesus gave a *new* law because the existing prohibitions on mistreatment of the poor, foreigners, widows, and orphans left "do not mistreat your fellow Israelite" as an unstated case. Since the Israelites were so prone to evil, and since Jesus came for the sinners rather than the righteous, he had to explicitly state that which was previously implicit: do not mistreat *anyone*. Now Paulites often cite Jesus' new command as the foundation for their heathen religion in which Satan is to be loved rather than hated and put to the sword.[267] In reality, Jesus' "new command" was already the most-repeated law in the Torah: do not mistreat people. Although Paulites generally agree that mistreatment is to be avoided, the prohibition on mistreatment greatly separates Christianity from the religion of the Pharisees who believed it was their piety compelling them to seek Jesus' murder.[268]

When Jesus says, "Do not mistreat one another," his meaning is stated more plainly than when the same is said in terms of love. The concise statement of what action is forbidden is superior to a broader statement about what sentiment is required. The difference between love and brotherly love is a subtle point to raise between neighbors, but the superiority of one convention to the other is amplified when Jesus commands that one should love his enemies.

Luke 6:27-28 (TTI)

27 "But to you who hear what I say: do not mistreat your enemies. Do good to them that hate you. 28 Bless those that curse you and pray for those who mistreat you.

In verse 28, the NIV references mistreatment directly making it clear that Jesus' teaching is in the context of the most-repeated commandment in the law of Moses: thou shall not mistreat. In verse 27, the NIV says, "Love your enemies," but this is vague and/or ambiguous bordering on oxymoronic. What is an enemy if not some-one excluded from one's love? The indeterminacy of this contradiction in terms is avoided completely when the Greek is translated in terms of mistreatment. Rephrased as such, Jesus restates a Proverb.

Luke 6:35 (KJV)

35 But love ye your enemies, and do good, and lend, hoping for nothing again; and your reward shall be great, and ye shall be the children of the Highest: for he is kind unto the unthankful and to the evil.

Proverbs 25:21-22 (KJV)

21 If thine enemy be hungry, give him bread to eat; and if he be thirsty, give him water to drink:

22 For thou shalt heap coals of fire upon his head, and the Lord shall reward thee.

Do not mistreat those who mistreat you. Being mistreated is not an excuse to mistreat. Answering a question raised in Matthew 5,[269] this is how Christians set themselves apart from pagans. This is what Christians do that is more than what others do.

Matthew 15:7-9 (NIV)

7 You hypocrites! Isaiah was right when he prophesied about you:

8 "'These people honor me with their lips,
   but their hearts are far from me.
9 They worship me in vain;
   their teachings are merely human rules.'"

As Jesus cited Leviticus when teaching that the Israelites must not mistreat one another,[270] here he refers to Isaiah.[271] Many such references in the Gospel show that Christ's intention was never to replace the old. He meant to preserve and restore it. The Pharisees bound themselves with human rules in Jesus' day and wrongly called themselves Jews, and now Paulites bind themselves with human rules to call themselves Christians. Some things never change, apparently, until one day they will. That day is the Day of the Lord.

If Isaiah was right and someone else was wrong, or if something else recorded in the law was wrong, Jesus' affinity for rebuke suggests that he would have specified which person was wrong or which written thing was wrong. Intending to trap Jesus into opposition to the law, the Pharisees once asked him about their intention to stone an adulterous woman to death.[272] If it was Jesus' intention to undermine the law, one assumes he would have done so given the opportunity. Even with such a perfect segue into phrasing a new religious doctrine, he never gave one. Instead, he said that whoever was without sin should cast the first stone. Jesus' message of compliance with the law of Moses is one of compassion and righteousness, and also that one must use his brain when studying God's word. Does it makes sense for someone to stone an adulteress to death when he himself has unredressed sins? Jesus' taught that compassion should be extended, and also that hypocrisy should be avoided. If the law says she should be put to death, that begs a question about who should kill her, and that question was not on the Pharisees' minds before Jesus brought it up. When he did, all of her accusers walked away: first the old and then the young.

The new commandment to love one another is said to be new material not found in the Old Testament. Jesus' instruction not to stone the adulteress is also said to be new. However, careful study reveals that the interaction with the adulteress is a retelling of the story of Judah and Tamar.[273] Judah wanted to kill Tamar when she became pregnant out of wedlock. Then he relented after learning that he was the father. He could not carry out the death sentence due to his hypocrisy. When he relented, he said, "She is more righteous than I."[274] When Nathan told David about a rich man that had taken a poor man's lamb, David ordered that the rich man should be put to death.[275] Then he learned that the Lord sent Nathan to indict him for killing Uriah and taking his wife. David said, "I have sinned against the Lord."[276]

John 7:24 (NIV)

24 ["]Stop judging by mere appearances, but instead judge correctly."

The law of the Lord is not a system of absolutes. Thinking is required. In the previous sections, we have considered the case for the dishonest word of the scribes in the Old Testament, and we have shown that the things written by Paul are riddled with falsehood. Should we assume that the English-translated Gospels are uniformly perfect? Hopefully, we have made the case to the reader by now that the perfection of God's word reflects God's purpose for it rather than the grammar, accuracy, and philosophical content of each word and phrase. Though the Word will achieve all that God has purposed for it,[277] at least the lack of a perfect English translation for *agape* tells us that the English versions of the Bible cannot *perfectly* reflect what was written in Greek many decades after Jesus had already left the Earth.

A discrepancy between the account of Judas Iscariot's death in Matthew[278] and that given in Acts[279] may only support the case for a problem in Acts beyond Jesus' questionable appearance to Saul,[280] but we must consider the case that even the Gospel is not without flaws. For example, at least a few picograms of external DNA matter must have joined with the 23 chromosomes in Mary's egg before Jesus could have a complete human genome, but this is not easily reconciled with the immaculate conception usually inferred from Matthew and Luke.[281] Even the case in which Mary may have maintained her virginity as the Holy Spirit came on her with in vitro fertilization or artificial insemination raises questions which require thinking. When Jesus tells about the end times in Matthew,[282] he says that not one stone will be left atop another in Jerusalem, and that his return will be like a flash of lighting. Then he tells his audience that their generation will not pass away before such things should happen. That generation has passed away already, so what can be the meaning? In John, Jesus asks, "If I want him to remain alive until I return, what's that to you?,"[283] so perhaps Jesus meant to preserve someone from that generation until his return. Whether or not the words in Matthew are wrong, the inference that the time until Jesus' return would be counted in decades cannot be the correct one.

In Matthew's account of Jesus' sermon on the mount, Jesus said that a man who looks at a woman in a certain way has committed adultery with her.[284] This statement deserves careful attention because it is strictly a New Testament idea that God hates sexuality and sexual activities under almost all circumstances. Such thinking has little to no basis in the Old Testament from which Jesus learned and taught, but it is prominent in modern Christian theology, to say the least. It is recorded in Genesis that God's sons saw (with their eyes, as in *looking*) that the human woman were beautiful and took any of them for wives that they chose.[285] It does not say that God's sons saw the human women and thought they would make good wives and caring mothers. Instead, God's sons saw their beauty and wanted to marry them. To the extent that sex is what usually distinguishes a wife from another woman, they wanted to have sex with them. Although many students of the Bible will cling dearly to their belief that Jesus said looking at a woman with lust is adultery, one must consider how God's sons might have looked at the human women to appreciate their beauty and desire sex without it being a lascivious sin. In the opinion this writer, looking at a woman, appreciating her beauty, and wanting to have sex with her cannot possibly be a sin in the absence of further circumstances. The claim that it is sinful is nearly as opposed to the norms established in the Old Testament as are many of Paul's false teachings. In fact, most will be hard-pressed to come up with a definition of *looks at with lust* that means something other than seeing the beauty and desiring sex. If a man walks past a magnificent tree and appreciates the beauty of the gnarly boughs swaying in the breeze, has he looked at the tree with lust to desire such a tree near his home? If the same man walks past a beautiful woman and gives her the same regard, has he committed a sin? The answer can only be no, on both counts.

When Judah looked at Tamar beside the road and wanted to have sex with who he thought was a prostitute, it was not recorded as a sin.[286] If not for Tamar disguising herself, as Satan had disguised himself when defrauding his father, and if not for Judah's severe mis-

239

treatment of her, both in getting her pregnant and then condemning her to death for what was as much his own action as it was hers, *and* in neglecting his obligation to wed her to his third son,[287] the story would have had almost no moral content to be recorded in the Bible at all. It is written that David was perfect in God's eyes except for one thing,[288] and that single thing was putting Bathsheba's husband to die on the front lines of battle. It was not the way David looked at Bathsheba. He looked at her and desired sexual relations with her, and God had no problem with it recorded in the Bible. When God later admonished David for his sin, he is paraphrased as saying, "David! If you wanted more women, I would have given you more women."[289] Such dialogue does not suggest that God frowns on sexualized looking. In fact, David's concubines were not his wives, and sex with non-wives is adultery under a standard of morality popular in the present day. Abraham's righteousness is praised throughout the Bible, but Hagar who bore his firstborn son was not his wife. What is sexual immorality, then? Breaking a woman's heart indicates mistreatment, and rape is a sin. Taking a woman's virginity might be an act of sinfulness depending on the circumstances. All of these would be sins of sexual immorality, but the umbrella of such immorality as it is imagined by many Christians today is too broad to be reconciled with the norms in the Bible.

There exists a sin called the lust of the flesh. Is this a desire for sexual affection? Or might it be the desire of the villain in Psalm 10 to lie in wait until he can drag an innocent soul away in his nets? If the lust of the wayward woman in Proverbs 7 is not one of the flesh, what is it? Based off little more than a single verse in Matthew 5, many students of the Bible find that sexual activity spans several lanes on the road that God has set himself against. If the law of the Lord is a prohibition on mistreatment, and if sex is very near to loving one another—the act is literally called making *love*—it is strange that God never says, "Do not kidnap people to rape and torture them to death in a hidden dungeon lair." Is it not more in line with the Word of God that the lust of the flesh describes something repugnant and far removed from making love? Fornication is another sin, but what word has been translated as *fornication* in the English? Near the end of Revelation, the great sin of the whore of Babylon is centered on her fornications and the filth of her adulteries.[290] A reasonable reader cannot infer that sex among unmarried couples is described. Neither can one study the Bible and find any evidence at all that sexual intercourse among the unmarried is evil in the eyes of the Lord. Abraham, David, Solomon, and many others engaged in fornication according to the strict definition of the word, and the Lord found no fault with them for it. Rather, the sin of fornication is sexualized to make it filthier in readers' minds. Service to false gods is called prostituting oneself to them for the same reason. Thus, the lust of flesh need not be inherently sexual. If Jesus taught that a man who looks at a woman and wants to rape her has already committed *adultery* with her, that is not a sin under God's prohibitions on sex. Rape is

241

a sin under God's prohibition on mistreatment. To the contrary, God likes it when people treat one another as they would like to be treated.

What can be the resolution to these things: the sexual things and the former things? We must ask in all cases, "What would Jesus do?" Jesus would search for answers in his knowledge of the Old Testament. If it is explicitly forbidden to mistreat widows, orphans, foreigners, and the poor, then it follows that mistreating one's fellow Israelite is also forbidden. The newness of Jesus' "new command" was a sad irony. Mistreating one's fellow man is not allowed, but one may use this context to paint a stereotypical caricature of what is called Judaism today. If one reads the Bible and says, "It doesn't say mistreating your neighbor is forbidden, so it must be allowed," then one is pejoratively said to be being *jewish*. This is the religious teaching of Satan, not Jesus. The lost sheep of Israel needed to have this spelled out for them plainly, and the descendants of those who accepted the message are called Christians today. Regarding negative stereotypes about those in the synagogue of Satan being deceitful tricksters, as was Israel long before them, consider the following from the Babylonian Talmud. It is written in Sanhedrin 76b and Sanhedrin 78a that if one sets a dog against another and the dog kills him, or if one sets a snake against another and the snake kills him, the one who set the dog or snake is exempt from punishment. It is written in Sanhedrin 77a that if someone ties up his neighbor and the neighbor dies of starvation, or if he incapacitates a man in the presence of a lion and the lion kills him, the man who was the perpetrator is not guilty of murder. Therefore, a glaring and obvious distinction is made between those who use the Old Testament supplemented with Talmudic nonsense as their religious source material and those who use the Old Testament supplemented with the Gospel and Revelation of Jesus Christ.

When a Canaanite woman asked Jesus to heal her daughter, he did not mistreat her.[291] He treated her as he would have liked to have been treated. He spoke to her frankly about his regard for her when he insinuated that she was like a dog begging at the Israelites' table, but he did not send the woman's daughter away unhealed. (God had commanded Moses to rid the land of Canaanites, and Joshua nearly did so.[292]) Jesus obeyed God's law and did not mistreat the foreigner. To the contrary, the Jews' Talmud says, "God is displeased when Jews show hospitality to gentiles."[293] It also says, "A non-Jew is not considered a neighbor,"[294] as if that somehow releases the Israelites from compliance with God's many commandments not to mistreat foreigners. Although God's prohibition on mistreatment is the central law in their Torah, they look for answers in the Talmuds that record nothing but their own opinions. As it is the central law in the Torah, the prohibition on mistreatment is also the central law in the religion of Jesus Christ. So, before asking if Jesus' message of love was really nothing but the golden rule,[295] one must first ask if the Israelites were really so wicked. To answer that question, one need look no further than the religious source material of today's

Talmudites: the literal and ideological descendants of the Pharisees who convinced the Romans to crucify Jesus. If the wickedness of Jesus' audience is not taken for granted, the simplicity of his message cannot be appreciated.

Jesus taught that the adulteress should not be killed even while it says in the Torah that adultery is punishable by death.[296] Critical thinking is required. Working on the Sabbath is punishable by death,[297] and yet Jesus healed on the Sabbath.[298] Therefore, it must be improper to read the Bible without acknowledging that the scribes' sparse words leave some things to the reader. Likewise, the translators behind the modern versions may not have known exactly what the words meant to begin with. Blind citation to scripture is not foolproof. It can foster impiety or even sacrilege. Blind citation was the tool of the Pharisees when they brought the adulteress before Jesus saying, "In the law commanded by Moses, she must be put to death." Unlike blind citation, the prohibition on mistreatment required by the golden rule *is* foolproof. It is self-evidently righteous. The religious axiom that one should treat another as he himself would like to be treated will stand up to any scrutiny. It is the true teaching of Christ. Where other words may fail, these words will never fail: "You will be my disciples if you treat each other how I have treated you."

The Christian church is thought to be an essential vehicle for Jesus' new religion despite him saying almost nothing about church in the Gospel. Church is not mentioned in Mark, Luke, or John, but the word appears twice in Matthew where we have found Jesus' misinterpreted remarks on the appreciation of a woman's physical beauty. The first reference to a church is as follows.

Matthew 16:16-27 (TTI)

16 Simon Peter answered, "You are the Messiah: the Living God as a younger man."

17 Jesus replied, "You are blessed, Simon son of Jonah, because this was not revealed to you by flesh and blood but by my later self in the future. 18 And I tell you that you are Peter, and upon this rock I will build my church, and the gates of Hades will not overcome it. 19 I will give you the keys to my kingdom in the future. Whatever you bind in the present will be bound in the future. Whatever you loose in the present shall be loosed in the future." 20 Then he ordered his disciples not to tell anyone that he was God Almighty as a younger man.

21 From that time forth, Jesus began to explain to his disciples that he must go to Jerusalem and suffer many things at the hands of the elders, the chief priests and the teachers of the law, and that he would be killed and raised to life on the third day. 22 Peter took him aside and began to rebuke him. "Never, Lord!" he said. "This will never happen to you!" 23 Jesus turned and said

to him, "Get behind me, Satan! You are a stumbling block to me. You are not concerned with heavenly things, but merely human concerns."

24 Then Jesus said to his disciples, "Anyone who wants to be my disciple must deny themselves and take up their cross to follow me. 25 Whoever wishes to save their life will lose it, but whoever loses their life for me will find it. 26 What good will it do a man if he gains the whole world only to forfeit his soul? Or what can a man give in exchange for his soul? 27 For the Son of Man is going to come in the glory of his future self, with his agents, and then he will repay each person according to what they have done.["]

Jesus did not evangelize the word of Paul. Only the church does that.[299] So, then, one must consider whether Jesus meant it in a good way when he told Peter that he would be the foundation of a church moments before calling him Satan and a stumbling block. The Paulite tradition that falsely claims fellowship with Christ is nothing if not a stumbling block for Jesus. The elevation of Paul's word over the Word and the Gospel perfectly reflects Jesus' rebuke to Peter in verse 23: Paulites are concerned with human things, not heavenly things.

In a study of Simon Peter, one notes that he denied Jesus in verse 22, and then, later, long after Jesus would *walk on water* to save him from sinking into the Sea of Galilee,[300] Peter would go on to become the denier, denying that he knew Jesus at all.[301]   As God changed Jacob's name to Israel by the Jabbok, Jesus changed Simon's name to Peter. Simon Peter is called the Rock, and what a rock does in water is sink straight to the bottom. Given the context for time travel, one must ask who Simon Peter was really and whether or not Jesus might have been calling him Satan in a figurative sort of way. Even Jesus' temptation by Satan in the wilderness is not so far removed from Peter telling Jesus that history would unfold other than as Jesus foretold in verse 21. One might say that Peter *tempted* Jesus not to go to Jerusalem.

Matthew, Mark, and Luke write that Jesus went from his baptism into the wilderness[302] while John writes that Jesus was with two of his disciples after the baptism.[303] This may not be a contradiction. One of the disciples was Andrew who asked Jesus where he was going.[304]   Jesus said, "Come and you'll see." Then Andrew brought his brother Peter to Jesus. This makes a decent case for Peter going with Jesus into the wilderness. When we were first introduced to Jacob and his brother Esau in Genesis, Esau was returning famished from *a hunt*.[305]   We supposed that Esau's identity as a man of the open country[306] would refer to time travel, so it is not too much to consider that Esau may have been near death when Jacob bought his birthright because he was returning from 40 days of fasting with Jesus. As a man of the open country in the usual sense, Esau would have been well qualified to accompany Jesus into the wilderness. Though it is written that Jacob was content to stay at home among the tents, he may have wondered later in his life where Esau was coming from on the day he sold his birthright. Possessing the ability to travel through time, he would have accompanied Esau and Jesus into the wilderness as Satan: Jacob as an older man. Certainly the four accounts of *heaven* being torn open at Jesus' baptism[307] should suggest that timelines intersected at the onset of his ministry. God announced his love for Jesus on that day, and then Satan was there too. He was with Jesus in the wilderness.

The Parable of the Weeds explains that God chose not to undo everything that Satan wrote into history. What was written would be left until the harvest, and this is the same authority granted to Peter in verse 19. Jesus plainly tells Peter that he will grant him the keys to the kingdom of *heaven* saying, "Whatever you bind in the present will be bound in the future." At Jesus' second and only other mention of a church,[308] he states again that anything which is bound or let loose *on earth* will also be bound or let loose *in heaven*. It is less clear that Jesus is speaking to Peter in the second reference to a church, but Peter immediately follows with a question, so it may be inferred that Jesus is reiterating his grant of temporal authorities to Peter. Casting Peter as Israel, Peter's question is suspicious. He asks how many times one should forgive a repeated sin.[309] If he was already hatching a new scheme for the nourishment of his excessive self-interest, as Israel would have been, then he may have asked Jesus how many times he'd be able to get away with it. In that case, Peter the apostle may have been Jacob the fraudster after he left the Bronze Age, but before he became Satan: the chief of the rebellion. Indeed, Satan might only have planted his weeds in history after gaining the authority to do so.

Luke 22:31-35 (NIV)

31 "Simon, Simon, Satan has asked to sift all of you as wheat. **32** But I have prayed for you, Simon, that your faith may not fail. And when you have turned back, strengthen your brothers."

33 But he replied, "Lord, I am ready to go with you to prison and to death."

34 Jesus answered, "I tell you, Peter, before the rooster crows today, you will deny three times that you know me."

35 Then Jesus asked them, "When I sent you without purse, bag or sandals, did you lack anything?"

When an argument broke out at the Last Supper over which of the apostles was to be considered greatest, Jesus may have called to Simon twice to tell him that Satan had started the argument. Given that Simon and Simon Peter were two different apostles, Jesus may have told Simon that Simon Satan had started the argument. Given the context for time travel, even a distinction among Simon and Simon Satan as alter egos of the same man at different times is something to be considered. Dialogue in John between Jesus and Peter references an unnamed disciple that Jesus loved.[310] When Peter asked, "What about him?.," Simon Satan may have asked Jesus about his earlier self when he was only Simon. He might have asked, "Now that I am defeated, you're not going to leave the filth of those things I wrote into history there, are you, Lord?" If Satan were at the Last Supper, it is consistent with our character study of Abraham's most famous grandson that he would seek to establish himself as the greatest among his peers. Today, the Chief Pharisee of the Catholic church is called the Successor to the Prince of the Apostles as if to insinuate that the outcome of the argument established Peter as the greatest.[311] In fact, Jesus said the endeavor to establish one apostle above the others was the endeavor of Satan. This message very much seems lost on the non-Levitical priests that populate the Vatican today.[312]

Verse 35 is usually thought to reference events in the Gospel, but it may reference Jacob's flight to Paddan Aram.[313] When Jacob had nothing along the way, he prayed, "Lord, you will be my God *if* you watch over me, and *if* if you give me food and clothes."[314] Perhaps Jesus meant to identify Peter as Satan (*again*) with this reference to the hasty escape from Beersheba after he lied about God giving him success in a hunt. When Jacob arrived at the edge of the Jabbok fleeing again from Laban, he called himself unworthy and prayed, "I left with only a staff, but now I have become two camps."[315]

God changed Jacob's name to Israel that day, and Jesus' alternating usage of the names Peter and Simon is evocative of God's alternating usage of the names Jacob and Israel earlier in Genesis. In the end, Peter the apostle denied knowing Jesus Christ three times as Jesus was condemned to death.

Matthew 10:33 (KJV)

33 But whosoever shall deny me before men, him will I also deny before my Father which is in heaven.

Peter's alleged upside down crucifixion is not recorded in the Bible, but there are references to his death.[316]

John 21:17-18 (NIV)

17 The third time he said to him, "Simon son of John, do you love me?"

Peter was hurt because Jesus asked him the third time, "Do you love me?" He said, "Lord, you know all things; you know that I love you."

Jesus said, "Feed my sheep. **18** Very truly I tell you, when you were younger you dressed yourself

---

> and went where you wanted; but when you are old you will stretch out your hands, and someone else will dress you and lead you where you do not want to go."

Israel dressed himself in goatskins to steal his older brother's blessing. The events by the river after he left Paddan Aram suggest that he was going only where he wanted after lying about God, again, when he told his wives about new instructions to depart from Laban's camp. Peter fits the bill on many counts, and this kind of catastrophic betrayal is well fitting in the battle of good versus evil. How evil is evil *really*, one might ask.

While many believe that Satan has almost no part in the Bible, he is probably as ubiquitous in the New Testament as he is in the Old. Like Paul and his false teachings which persist in the world to the present day, Peter's church may be purposed to undermine Jesus and deceive those who would be his sheep. The appearance of Satan rather than Jesus when Paul was going to Damascus will better account for Paul's rebellious instruction than the commonly accepted version of events. Paul had never heard Jesus' voice, so he would have had no way to know who was speaking. If Israel would lie about what God's commands were, would he not lie about who God was? If he would tell his father that he was Esau,[317] would he not tell Saul that he was Jesus? When Paul refers to "the new creation,"[318] that may be what is commonly called "the Satanic rebellion." During the Israelite monarchy, the rebellious northern kingdom was damned for appointing anyone as priests, even though they were not Levites.[319] The continuation of the non-Levitical priesthood is unbroken from the Kingdom of Israel until today, and the fact of this matter highlights the false prophecy Israel gave on his deathbed. He foretold that the Levites would become an unremarkable tribe scattered for their violence before God made them into his priests. To this day, Peter's church continues in Israel's sin, and many of the children of Satan continue in the tradition of deception of their father via the political power afforded to them through the governing bodies of the Vatican.

The company of God, his angels, and Satan at the beginning of Job[320] may be the same given in the New Testament as Jesus, the apostles, and Peter. Though it is not written in the Bible that Satan was a high ranking angel fallen from grace, this is exactly what is written if Peter is Satan. Most cuttingly, we suggested in Section 9 that God's curse on the serpent in the Garden of Eden should be read as, "Eat my dust, Satan." The etymology of this phrase is found in the American west where one cowboy might tell another cowboy to take his horse to the rear. The saying means, "Get behind me."[321] It is *exactly* what Jesus said to Peter when he called him Satan.[322]

To further question whether a good thing was referenced by Jesus' non-instructive reference to an establishment that would later be called *a church* when his words were translated into English, consider Jesus' instruction on piety.

Matthew 6:1 (NIV)

1 "Be careful not to practice your righteousness in front of others to be seen by them. If you do, you will have no reward from your Father in heaven.["]

In this regard, the Catholic church whose Pope sits in the gilt Throne of Saint Peter teaches rebellion against Christ far exceeding even that taught by Paul.

Matthew 6:6-8 (KJV)

6 But thou, when thou prayest, enter into thy closet, and when thou hast shut thy door, pray to thy Father which is in secret; and thy Father which seeth in secret shall reward thee openly.

7 But when ye pray, use not vain repetitions, as the heathen do: for they think that they shall be heard for their much speaking.

8 Be not ye therefore like unto them: for your Father knoweth what things ye have need of, before ye ask him.

As Matthew 6 continues, Jesus will give the Lord's prayer as a template for communion with God.[323] He says that one should ask for God's will to be done in the present as it is in the future. To the contrary, Peter did not want Jesus to go to Jerusalem. When it is written in Genesis that Esau's birthright was detestable to him,[324] perhaps that was similar to Peter's feeling when he said, "Never Lord! This will never happen to you!"[325] In the present day, the so-called Supreme Pontiff of the Universal Church does not heed Jesus' teachings on prayer at all. Instead, the repetitive chanting of Latin prayers is a pillar of the Roman Catholic church even while there is little reason to think Jesus might have spoken Latin or heard a word of Latin in his life from someone other than the Romans that crucified him. Since the Romans did crucify him, would he want his church to be called Roman? Or would he want it emphasized that the Romans were a stumbling block to him? Did Jesus come for the lost sheep of Israel, and the lost sheep of Rome? In what way is praying the rosary different from what the heathen do?

Jesus did mention a church in Matthew twice, but it is not clear at all that his words imply an intent to create a new religion or to abolish God's covenant with the Israelites. In fact, that implication is fully contrived. It exists only in the minds of those who want it to be true. In 1517, Martin Luther did Christendom a great service when he posted his Ninety-Five Theses on a church in Germany. His protest against the absurdities of the Roman Catholic church and the lack of good faith between their priesthood and the Bible made way for the Protestant Reformation. Due to Luther's careful study of the

Bible and his valid conclusions, modern man might be blessed to hear about a personal relationship with Jesus Christ that is church-free and very far removed from Catholic priests as non-Levitical intercessors for the Lord. No fault can be found in the organization of a Christian social club for evangelism and study, but incorrect dogmas persist even in Protestant churches. The born again tradition in the Southern Baptist church is one such example. If being *born again* through the statement of a single prayer on a Sunday morning is the only way into heaven, and if the alternative to heaven is hell, then everyone would have gone to hell until that tradition was invented, at minimum. Although Baptist theology treats the Word of God with infinitely greater respect than does Catholic theology, blind citation to a few idiomatic expressions about being born again[326] will be a defect in one's walk with Christ.

John 3:1-3 (NIV)

1 Now there was a Pharisee, a man named Nicodemus who was a member of the Jewish ruling council. 2 He came to Jesus at night and said, "Rabbi, we know that you are a teacher who has come from God. For no one could perform the signs you are doing if God were not with him."

3 Jesus replied, "Very truly I tell you, no one

can see the kingdom of God unless they are born again."

John 11:25-26 (NIV)

25 Jesus said to her, "I am the resurrection and the life. The one who believes in me will live, even though they die; 26 and whoever lives by believing in me will never die. Do you believe this?"

Jesus requires more than a pre-packaged prayer. One must *live* by believing in him. He promised to return and repay each person according to what they have done,[327] but no realistic Bible study can find that Christ's judgment will hinge solely on whether or not certain words were honestly repeated. However, like salesmen asking to buy when emotion is high, born again church service ends with a promise that the fate of one's immortal soul depends on nothing more than a prayer and a moment of honest belief. A better appraisal of Jesus' words in verse 26 suggests that belief is determined by actions, not lip service or even the most earnest and heartfelt lip service. After all, Peter told Jesus that he loved him three times,[328] and he may have meant it when he said it.

To continue to dispel the notion that Christians ought to follow a different religion than Jesus followed, or that Jesus terminated God's covenant with the Israelites in favor of a new one, consider Luke's account of the last supper.

Luke 22:8-20 (KJV)

8 And he sent Peter and John, saying, Go and prepare us the passover, that we may eat.

9 And they said unto him, Where wilt thou that we prepare?

10 And he said unto them, Behold, when ye are entered into the city, there shall a man meet you, bearing a pitcher of water; follow him into the house where he entereth in.

11 And ye shall say unto the goodman of the house, The Master saith unto thee, Where is the guestchamber, where I shall eat the passover with my disciples?

12 And he shall shew you a large upper room furnished: there make ready.

13 And they went, and found as he had said unto them: and they made ready the passover.

14 And when the hour was come, he sat down, and the twelve apostles with him.

15 And he said unto them, With desire I have desired to eat this passover with you before I suffer:

16 For I say unto you, I will not any more eat thereof, until it be fulfilled in the kingdom of God.

17 And he took the cup, and gave thanks, and said, Take this, and divide it among yourselves:

18 For I say unto you, I will not drink of the fruit of the vine, until the kingdom of God shall come.

19 And he took bread, and gave thanks, and brake it, and gave unto them, saying, This is my body which is given for you: this do in remembrance of me.

20 Likewise also the cup after supper, saying, This cup is the new testament in my blood, which is shed for you.

The new testament in Jesus' blood, also translated as the new *covenant*, is not identified in the scripture. Rather, the popular meaning of verse 20 is inferred. Students of the Bible—or students of Peter and Paul—will sometimes say, "The only thing that Jesus might have reasonably meant in referring to a new covenant in his blood was that the old one would to be nailed to the cross." Sometimes the clear implication of Jesus' words is said to be that the old covenant would be terminated with Jesus' life replacing the Passover lamb. Neither of these conclusions is obvious to this writer, but the purpose of the time travel interpretation of the Bible is to make room for new conclusions.

259

Consider Jesus' words about not eating or drinking until the Kingdom of God comes. A common interpretation for these words supposes that Jesus' crucifixion would mark the coming of that kingdom and the fulfillment of God's covenant with the Israelites. Since the Kingdom of God is in the future, another interpretation is that Jesus intended to leave Jerusalem via time travel, and he would not eat or drink again until he was in the future. Jesus had already made it known that he would be raised from the dead in three days time,[329] so he may have spoken about the agents of the Kingdom of God coming from the future to rescue or resurrect him. We have suggested that God's process is one of iterative development by smooth deformations, so the revision of Jesus' timeline from death onto life might have moved him from death to resurrection and then rescue. Ultimately, Jesus will avoid the cross altogether in a second coming. In the interim, Jesus may have left the tomb by ascent into the future where he would be healed with the kind of technologies that Ezekiel saw in the valley of dry bones.[330] Only at that time would he break his fast and taste wine again.

The appearance of deceased holy men[331] at the moment of Jesus' death suggests that they may have arrived by time travel from the times at which they were alive. These risen holy men seen in Jerusalem may have been the same great army that Ezekiel saw raised in the valley. God may have rewound them from death onto life as a first step in rewinding Jesus from betrayal into victory. Going so far as to speculate that God may have shown Ezekiel the valley of dry bones on the day of Jesus' crucifixion, we should also recall God's words at the commission of Isaiah. God said, "Make the heart of this people calloused, make their ears dull, and close their eyes."[332] God seems very much to have desired that the Israelites should be healed by Jesus' message, but he told Isaiah to prophecy blindness and deafness so they would never understand and never perceive, lest their hearts be healed. This discrepancy in God' intention may be avoided if his forgiveness stopped when they killed Jesus, and then he spoke to Isaiah after that. Perhaps Jesus' murder was the final straw.

Jesus' reference to a new covenant in his blood has other interpretations than the usual ones. To the extent that one might restrict one's study to *reasonable* interpretations, it is hoped that the reader will not consider the Paulite establishment of a new covenant to be reasonable. The Day of the Judgment must come so God can fulfill the terms of the existing covenant: terms of life and terms of death.[333] God's work of ages has been to bring forth his kingdom through a protected bloodline, and that post-Biblical monarchy is where the new covenant will be established. In the sense of the continuation of Jesus' life beyond the cross, the new covenant in his blood will be a glorious, heavenly kingdom much unlike the disastrous world left in the wake of his crucifixion. When the Gospel of Jesus Christ is a retelling of God's journey toward physical lordship over all mankind, the new covenant is very much *in the blood* of Jesus Christ. The new covenant comes in the blood of Jesus' life, not his death. It will come when the current covenant is completed at the time of the harvest: the second coming.

Notes

[261]E.g.: Matthew 16:1-4, Matthew 22:15-22, Mark 11:15-18, Mark 12:13-17, Luke 2:41-47, Luke 20:20-26, John 7:14-15, John 8:3-11, etc.

[262]Leviticus 19:18.

[263]Deuteronomy 10:19.

[264]Exodus 20, Deuteronomy 5.

[265]E.g.: Exodus 22:21-24, Leviticus 19:15, Leviticus 19:33-34, Numbers 20:14-16, Deuteronomy 24:17-18, Deuteronomy 27:19, etc.

[266]E.g.: Exodus 22:25-27, Deuteronomy 14:28-29, Deuteronomy 24:19-22, etc.

[267]In Matthew 10:34, Jesus says, "I did not come to bring peace, but a sword." The sword clearly has a place in Christianity, but Paulite thinking allows almost no place for one. The nearest to a sword one might get in the Paulite tradition is a figurative one equipped in the whole armor of God, as in Ephesians 6:10-18.

[268]E.g.: Matthew 12:14, Mark 11:18, Luke 4:28-30, John 5:18, John 7:1, etc.

[269]Matthew 5:47.

[270]Matthew 5:43, Mark 12:31.

[271]Isaiah 29:13.

[272]John 8:1-11.

[273]Genesis 38:1-10.

[274]Genesis 38:26.

[275]2 Samuel 12:1-7.

[276]2 Samuel 12:13-14.

[277]Isaiah 55:10-11.

[278]Matthew 27:1-5.

[279]Acts 1:18.

[280]Acts 9:1-9.

[281]Matthew 1:20, Luke 1:26-38. It is notable that the angel Gabriel tells Mary in Luke 1:37 that no word from God will ever fail because Paul will insist many times in the remainder of the New Testament that God's promise of an everlasting covenant in the flesh failed.

[282]Matthew 24.

[283]John 21:22

[284]Matthew 5:28.

[285]Genesis 6:1-2.

[286]To further support our thesis that the strictly Puritanical view on God's regard for sex does not reflect the norms in the Bible, consider that prostitutes are not so poorly regarded in the scripture. Most often, God's disdain for prostitution regards prostituting oneself to false gods, e.g.: Exodus 34:15-16, Leviticus 17:7, Leviticus 20:5-6, Judges 2:17, Judges 8:33, Hosea 5:3-4, etc. Many of God's harshest words against prostitution are spoken against cities turning to evil, e.g.: Isaiah 1:21, Ezekiel 16:15-18, Nahum 3:4, etc. In fact, a fair reading suggests that it is whorishness which God hates. Regarding the act itself, God certainly makes it clear that it is not good. Deuteronomy 23:17-18 records that no Israelite may become a prostitute, and that the Lord hates the wages of a prostitute. The Lord promotes family values in Leviticus 19:29 when he forbids parents from putting their children into prostitution, but the only time a prostitute must be put to death is when she is a priest's daughter, as in Leviticus 21:9. Since the Levitical priests were a wealthy class, a priest's daughter would not be compelled to prostitute herself by the harsh economic realities that one might assume in most cases. Rather, her intention would be in some part to disgrace her father. The prohibitions on priests marrying prostitutes in Leviticus 21:7-9 leave out the case of relations between non-priests and prostitutes. Among 100 or more mentions of prostitution in the Bible, none of them damns a woman for simple prostitution. To the contrary, God in Hosea 1:1-2 orders Hosea to marry a promiscuous woman and have children with her even as a prophet is seemingly holier than a priest. Perhaps the wisdom of Solomon most concisely states the reality: Proverbs 6:26

263

teaches that a prostitute can be had for a loaf of bread while another man's wife preys on one's life. "Why sin when you can hire a prostitute?," Solomon asks. Although a wiser question about why one would seek a prostitute rather than a caring partner in mutual affection is too plain to be recorded in Proverbs where it calls hiring prostitutes a waste of money (Proverbs 29:3), Proverbs, as a matter of realistic practicality, does not cast prostitution as an inherently sinful endeavor.

287 Genesis 38:6-11.

288 1 Kings 15:5.

289 2 Samuel 12:8.

290 Revelation 17:3-6, Revelation 18:1-5.

291 Matthew 15:21-28.

292 Deuteronomy 20:16-17, Joshua 10:40.

293 BT Sanhendrin 104a.

294 BT Sanhedrin 52b.

295 Matthew 7:12.

296 Leviticus 20:10.

297 Exodus 35:2.

298 Matthew 12:9-14, Mark 3:1-6, Luke 6:6-11, Luke 13:10-17, John 7:21-23.

299 Church is referenced about 100 times in Paul's letters, e.g.: 1 Corinthians 4:16-17, 1 Corinthians 7:17, 1 Corinthians 12:28, 1 Corinthians 14:12, 1 Corinthians 14:26-40, Galatians 1:21-23, Ephesians 3:10, Colossians 1:24, 1 Timothy 3:14-15, 1 Timothy 5:17, etc.

300 Matthew 14:28-31.

301 Matthew 26:69-75, Mark 14:66-72, Luke 22:54-62, John 18:15-18, John 15:25-27.

302 Matthew 3:13-17, Matthew 4:1-11, Mark 1:9-13, Luke 3:21-22, Luke 4:1-13.

303 John 1:29-35.

304 John 1:37-42.

305 Genesis 25:29-30.

306 Genesis 25:27.

307 E.g.: Mark 1:10-11.

[308]Matthew 18:15-20.

[309]Matthew 18:21-22.

[310]John 21:2-23.

[311]Since Peter is called Satan in Matthew 16:23 and Mark 8:33, one might call the Pope the Successor to the Prince of Darkness.

[312]God says in Genesis 2:18 that it is not good for man to be alone. This message also seems lost in the Vatican where a vow of celibacy is thought to be some form of godliness, or is thought to be in some way pleasing to the Lord.

[313]Jesus' hope in Luke 22:32 that Peter should strengthen his brothers may refer to his brother Esau who would go on to sell his birthright in a moment of weakness.

[314]Genesis 28:20-21.

[315]Genesis 32:10.

[316]E.g.: 2 Peter 1:12-15.

[317]Genesis 27:24.

[318]2 Corinthians 5:17, Galatians 6:15.

[319]1 Kings 12:31.

[320]Job 1:6.

[321]A skeptical reader might believe that God's curse on the serpent was taken to mean, "Eat my dust," in anticipation of a citation to this dialogue between Jesus and Peter. In fact, the first edition of this book concluded with 19 sections and made no such citation to the command, "Get behind me." The likeness between God's curse on the serpent and Jesus' rebuke to Peter was discovered only during the preparation of a second edition including a twentieth section on the nature of Christianity.

[322]Matthew 16:23, Mark 8:33.

[323]Matthew 6:9-13.

[324]Genesis 25:34.

[325]Matthew 16:22.

[326]E.g.: 1 Peter 1:3, 1 Peter 1:23.

[327]Matthew 16:27.

[328]John 21:15-17.

[329]Matthew 17:22-23, Mark 8:31-32, Luke 9:22.

[330]Ezekiel 37:1-14.

265

[331] Matthew 27:52-53.
[332] Isaiah 6:9-10.
[333] Deuteronomy 27-30, Exodus 20-23.

Jeremiah 5:31 (NIV)

31 The prophets prophesy lies,
   the priests rule by their own authority,
and my people love it this way.
   But what will you do in the end?

Made in the USA
Middletown, DE
10 October 2023

40300116R00168